Cambridge Elements

Elements in Environmental, Natural Resource and Sustainable Development Economics
edited by
Phoebe Koundouri
Athens University of Economics and Business (Greece) &
University of Cambridge (UK)

THE SPATIAL DIMENSION IN ENVIRONMENTAL AND RESOURCE ECONOMICS

William Brock
University of Wisconsin, Madison
and University of Missouri, Columbia

Anastasios Xepapadeas
Athens University of Economics and Business
and University of Bologna

Shaftesbury Road, Cambridge CB2 8EA, United Kingdom

One Liberty Plaza, 20th Floor, New York, NY 10006, USA

477 Williamstown Road, Port Melbourne, VIC 3207, Australia

314–321, 3rd Floor, Plot 3, Splendor Forum, Jasola District Centre,
New Delhi – 110025, India

Cambridge University Press is part of Cambridge University Press & Assessment,
a department of the University of Cambridge.

We share the University's mission to contribute to society through the pursuit of
education, learning and research at the highest international levels of excellence.

www.cambridge.org
Information on this title: www.cambridge.org/9781009694391

DOI: 10.1017/9781009694407

First published 2026

A catalogue record for this publication is available from the British Library

*A Cataloging-in-Publication data record for this Element is available from the Library
of Congress*

ISBN 978-1-009-69439-1 Hardback
ISBN 978-1-009-69438-4 Paperback
ISSN 2977-747X (online)
ISSN 2977-7461 (print)

The Spatial Dimension In Environmental And Resource Economics

Elements in Environmental, Natural Resource and Sustainable Development Economics

DOI: 10.1017/9781009694407
First published online: April 2026

William Brock
University of Wisconsin, Madison and University of Missouri, Columbia

Anastasios Xepapadeas
Athens University of Economics and Business and University of Bologna

Author for correspondence: Anastasios Xepapadeas, xepapad@aueb.gr

Abstract: Although the spatial dimension is embedded in most issues studied by environmental and resource economics, its incorporation into economic models is not widespread. As a result, significant aspects of important problems remain hidden, which could lead to policy failures. This Element fills this gap by exploring how space can be integrated into environmental and resource economics. The emergence of spatial patterns in economic models through Turing's mechanism is explained and an extension of Pontryagin's maximum principle under spatial dynamics is provided. Examples of the use of spatial dynamics serve to illustrate why space matters in environmental policy design. Moreover, the differentiation of policy when spatial transport mechanisms are considered is made clear. The tools presented, along with their applications, provide foundations for future research in spatial environmental and resource economics in which the underlying spatial dimension – which is very real – is fully taken into account.

Keywords: environmental economics, spatial dimension, spatial dynamics, spatial pattern formation, environmental policy

ISBNs: 9781009694391 (HB), 9781009694384 (PB), 9781009694407 (OC)
ISSNs: 2977-747X (online), 2977-7461 (print)

Contents

1 Introduction

Space is a central feature in the study of the environment and natural resources since air pollutants are transported in the atmosphere from the source of their emissions via turbulent eddy motion and winds, heat is transported from the equator toward the poles, and resources diffuse in space, usually moving from high- to low-concentration locations. In terms of the natural sciences, the spatial dimension relates mainly to the study of mechanisms that explain the emergence of spatial patterns in nature, such as polar amplification (i.e., the spatial pattern of the temperature anomaly[1]), stripes or spots on animal coats, the spatial distribution of the brown cloud in South Asia and the Indian Ocean, and many others (e.g., Ramanathan et al., 2002; Cantrell and Cosner, 2003; Murray, 2003; Hoyle, 2006; Bekryaev et al., 2010). Deacon et al. (1998: 387) point out that "The temporal dimension of resource use is not the only one that matters. . . . the spatial pattern of natural resource use may affect the value of environmental service flows in ways that existing analysis often ignores. Clearly, important research opportunities lie at the nexus of natural resources and the environment." The purpose of this Element is to bring the spatial dimension into environmental and resource economics and, by combining it with the temporal dimension, to provide an integrated approach to environmental and resource economics in a spatiotemporal context.

In economics, the spatial dimension has been analyzed extensively in the context of new economic geography. There is a large body of literature studying agglomerations and clusters in various spatial scales, as a result of interactions between scale economies and spatial spillovers.[2] Moreover, a strand of literature on spatial growth theory has emerged which studies the spatiotemporal characteristics of economic growth under spatial knowledge spillovers or capital diffusion.[3]

---

[1] Temperature anomaly is the change in temperature relative to a given benchmark temperature. Polar amplification describes the phenomenon wherein surface temperature change at high latitudes exceeds the global average surface temperature change (IPCC, 2021). The terms Arctic amplification or Antarctic amplification are used when describing the phenomenon occurring at just one of the poles.

[2] See, for example, Krugman (1996, 1998), Fujita et al. (1999), Lucas and Rossi-Hansberg (2002), Quah (2002), Baldwin et al. (2003), Baldwin and Martin (2004), Fujita and Mori (2005), Ioannides and Overman (2007), Desmet and Rossi-Hansberg (2010), Fujita and Thisse (2013), Brock et al. (2014d), and Redding and Rossi-Hansberg (2017).

[3] See, for example, Quah (1996, 1997), Boucekkine et al. (2009), Desmet and Rossi-Hansberg (2009), Boucekkine et al. (2013), Brock et al. (2014a), Xepapadeas and Yannacopoulos (2016, 2023), Boucekkine et al. (2019b), Gozzi and Leocata (2022), Augeraud-Véron et al. (2024), Tsangaris et al. (2024).

When the spatial features characterizing the environment and natural resources are combined with the activities of economic agents that – acting as forward-looking optimizing producers or consumers – interact with the environment, a number of new issues emerge. These issues are not captured by the traditional approach of environmental and resource economics, which, in most cases, does not account for the underlying spatial dimension.[4]

Pigouvian taxes, which internalize the environmental externality, or cap-and-trade policies and tradable emissions permits, which try to substitute for the missing markets for environmental goods such as clean air, are the standard instruments of environmental policy. In resource management, landing taxes are used to control commercial fisheries. When space is not taken into account, the optimal price instrument (tax) or the optimal quantity instrument (permits) is derived as a solution of a social welfare maximization problem with the underlying assumption that the spatial diffusion of the externality is infinite and therefore the externality is uniform in space. This in turn implies that spatially uniform policy instruments will be used to correct for the externality.

In reality, however, the diffusion of the environmental externalities is not infinite. This could generate spatial patterns for the externality which range from local scales such as differences in local ambient pollution, to global scales related to problems such as acid rain (with different acid depositions in different locations) or polar amplification, which induces different magnitudes of the temperature anomaly across the globe. Furthermore, the interaction of diffusive environmental externalities with mechanisms generating economic agglomerations and clustering introduces new elements which should be accounted for in policy design. In a similar way, renewable resources move in space and generate spatial patterns or clusters as their movement is taken into account in harvesting decisions.

When diffusive externalities are present, then spatially uniform Pigouvian taxes might not be optimal. That is, instruments under the assumption of perfect mixing and spatial homogeneity might be different from the optimal instruments that take into account spatial diffusion. This could lead to the need for localized Pigouvian taxes or cap-and-trade policies. Moreover, when the diffusive externalities interact with economic centipedal or centrifugal forces, more instruments in addition to Pigouvian taxes or cap-and-trade policies might be necessary. Acemoglu et al. (2016) have argued that additional instruments are

---

[4]   Some exceptions are, for example, Kaitala et al. (1992), Mäler and de Zeeuw (1998), Sanchirico and Wilen (1999, 2005), Goetz and Zilberman (2000, 2007), Smith and Wilen (2003), Xabadia et al. (2004), Brock and Xepapadeas (2005, 2008, 2010), Sanchirico (2005), Wilen (2007), Smith et al. (2009), Brock et al. (2013), Brock et al. (2014b), and Cai et al. (2023).

needed in the context of climate change. They argue that when dirty and green technologies compete in production, a carbon tax is not sufficient to correct for the climate externality; subsidies to encourage production and innovation in green technologies are also required.

An important characteristic of diffusive externalities relates to the interaction between the spatial dimension and the temporal dimension. Environmental and resource management problems are analyzed mostly in a dynamic context. When spatial diffusion is introduced, novel issues emerge. For example, does spatial diffusion of the environmental externality induce the evolution of spatial patterns? Is it optimal to support spatial patterns or is it optimal to suppress them and seek convergence to spatially homogeneous outcomes? What is the appropriate policy instrument or menu of policy instruments for attaining these objectives?

Ambiguity and model misspecification concerns, along with aversion to ambiguity, are emerging as important issues in both theory and policy design (Hansen and Sargent, 2001, 2008; Hansen et al., 2006). These issues are especially important in the context of climate change, where large ambiguities regarding process and impacts exist and model misspecification raises issues regarding the reliability of policies derived from such models (Pindyck, 2007, 2011, 2012, 2013; Brock and Hansen, 2019). With a diffusive externality such as heat transport toward the poles, ambiguity acquires a spatial structure because aversion to ambiguity could be different across locations, while misspecification concerns could be very important for high-impact locations (hot spots). In this case, policy design under ambiguity and misspecification concerns needs to account for the spatial dimension using methods such as robust control.

The arguments presented above suggest that the study of diffusive environmental externalities and spatial spillovers is important in order to understand their interactions with the economy and the mechanisms generating endogenously spatial patterns in coupled systems of the economy and the environment, and to design the appropriate regulatory instruments to control them. The purpose of this Element is threefold: to present ways to model spatial transport mechanisms and the emerging spatial (or diffusive) externalities and to incorporate them into dynamic, forward-looking optimizing economic models; to explore the potential endogenous emergence of optimal spatial patterns under diffusive externalities; and to present policy instruments for controlling them.

The study of diffusive externalities or resources in a dynamic optimization framework with continuous space requires the extension of standard optimal control methods in which dynamic constraints are represented by ordinary differential equations (ODEs) to the case in which the dynamic constraints are partial differential equations (PDEs) or integrodifferential equations (IDEs). We present a heuristic extension of Pontryagin's principle for solving these problems, which could be a useful tool for economists studying these issues.[5]

When the analysis is extended to spatiotemporal domains, a central issue in the natural sciences is the way in which reaction-diffusion systems could generate patterns in space. Alan Turing, in his seminal paper (Turing, 1952), showed how diffusion could generate spatial patterns. The Turing mechanism requires a system of at least two interacting state variables and its applications in the context of new economic geography (Krugman, 1996, 1998)[6] were not directly linked to explicit dynamic optimization. The Turing mechanism has been extended to optimizing spatiotemporal systems with diffusive externalities by Brock and Xepapadeas (2008), with results suggesting that diffusion can generate spatial patterns in the quantity-shadow value space (or state-costate space), which is equivalent to pattern generation in the state-control space. This result raises issues related to optimal pattern formation, differences in spatial patterning between socially optimal and market solutions, and the design of optimal spatially dependent policy instruments.

This Element is organized into two main parts. The first part (Sections 2, 3, and 4) provides theoretical foundations which are necessary for a holistic understanding of the applications which use this theory. Section 2 presents approaches for modeling spatial transport in continuous and discrete space. Section 3 links descriptive spatiotemporal dynamics with optimization by providing an extension of Pontryagin's maximum principle to optimal control problems which are constrained by spatiotemporal dynamics. Section 4 builds on the results from Section 3 to study the emergence of spatial patterns in optimizing spatiotemporal models, extending in this way the concept of Turing's spatial instability. In addition, this section provides an introduction to spatiotemporal optimization in cooperative and noncooperative settings.

The second part provides applications of optimal management and policy design under diffusive externalities and spatial spillovers, along with additional theoretical results that enhance our understanding of the mechanisms

---

[5] It should be noted that when the space is discrete (i.e., when we have patches with dispersion of populations, or pollutants across patches), then dynamic optimization involves a set of ODEs, one for each patch (see, for example, Smith et al. [2009], as well as Section 5.1 in this Element). In continuous space the dimensionality is drastically reduced, although the difficulty of solving a dynamic optimization problem with PDEs as constraints is added. Furthermore, as will be shown in Section 4, the mechanism generating spatial patterns and agglomerations is better exposed, and it is possible to incorporate more complex mechanisms for modeling spatial transport that emerge in the context of climate change.

[6] Krugman used Turing's method to explain the generation of agglomerations in the 12-region racetrack model.

underlying the applications. Results related to areas in which spatial economics is important – fisheries management, groundwater management, pollution control, urban economics, and infectious diseases – are presented in Section 5. Section 6 studies the regulation of transboundary and global externalities in the spatiotemporal domain. It focuses on transboundary pollution regulation as well as spatial models of climate change, which are gaining increasing attention in the literature as the spatial heterogeneity of climate change impacts becomes more evident. Section 7 introduces spatially structured uncertainty and presents robust control methods in a spatial setting. Section 8 offers some closing remarks; technical material and proofs are provided in the Appendices.

PART I THEORY

2 Modeling Spatial Transport

The spatial dimension and the transport of all kinds of things across locations – whether they are environmental variables such as pollutants, water, animals, and vegetation, or economic variables such as capital, labor, and knowledge – can be incorporated into models in various ways. Implicit representations could assign weights associated with a spatial scale or describe the part of the spatial domain occupied by a certain type of population. Explicit representations treat space either as a continuum or as a collection of discrete patches and define a mechanism that characterizes the movements across patches. We describe some of the more important mechanisms in this section.[7]

2.1 Diffusion

A central concept in any attempt to model the movement of variables associated with environmental and natural resources in continuous space is the concept of diffusion. A diffusion process describes a situation in which movements of individual objects such as pollutants or animals result in a regular macroscopic flow. Diffusion models can be derived from dispersal models of random walks, from Fick's law, or from stochastic differential equations. Fick's law states that in one-dimensional space (that is, a line), diffusion moves objects from locations of high concentration to locations of low concentration. If the concentration of a material at time $t \geq 0$ and spatial point $x \in \mathcal{O} \subseteq \mathbb{R}$, where $\mathcal{O}$ is the spatial domain, is denoted by $y(t, x)$, then Fick's law states that the flux J of the material is proportional to the gradient (that is, the derivative with

---

[7] For a more detailed description of these mechanisms, see Murray (2003) and Cantrell and Cosner (2003). See also Smith et al. (2009) who present linear diffusion processes and dispersion processes in discrete space and discuss applications to renewable resource management.

respect to space $\frac{\partial y(t,x)}{\partial x}$) of the material, or $J \propto -\frac{\partial y(t,x)}{\partial x}$, $J = -D\frac{\partial y(t,x)}{\partial x}$. If the material's net growth in a spatial location is determined by $f(y(t,x), u(t,x))$, then concentration dynamics under diffusion are given by the PDE[8]

$$\frac{\partial y(t,x)}{\partial t} = f(y(t,x), u(t,x)) + D\frac{\partial y^2(t,x)}{\partial x^2}, \ y(0,x) = y_0(x). \tag{1}$$

In (1), D is called diffusivity and is a constant indicating that the diffusion is linear. Diffusivity, as we will see later on in this section, could depend on the location or the concentration itself in the context of nonlinear diffusion. This is important in the context of one- and two-dimensional models of heat diffusion toward the poles (e.g., North, 1975a, 1975b; Ghil, 1976; North et al., 1981; North and Kim, 2017). The function $u(t,x)$ represents a control, such as harvesting, emissions, or abatement. Equation (1), apart from the temporal initial condition, should be supplemented with spatial boundary conditions which provide information about what the concentration is expected to be at the boundary of the spatial domain $\mathcal{O}$ at all times.[9]

If we consider a vector $\mathbf{y} = (y_1, \ldots, y_n)$ of concentrations at time t and location x, which diffuse with diffusivities $\mathbf{D} = (D_1, \ldots, D_n)$ and interact among themselves, and a vector of controls $\mathbf{u} = (u_1, \ldots, u_n)$, then (1) will represent a reaction-diffusion system. The Fickian diffusion framework can be further extended to include an advection term that represents a drift in the process caused by external forcing such as wind or currents (Murray, 2003; Wilen, 2007). In this case, the advection term $-V(\partial y(t,x)/\partial x)$ is added to the right-hand side of (1).

Figure 1 presents the spatiotemporal evolution of resource biomass under linear diffusion.[10]

Figure 1 indicates that the role of diffusion is to generate a spatially heterogeneous pattern of concentration. In our example, this spatial pattern seems to persist over time. Persistent spatial heterogeneity raises policy questions regarding the need to design spatially heterogeneous policies if the emerging spatial pattern is not the desired one.

---

[8] For the derivation and for extensions to higher dimension spatial domains, see Brock et al. (2014b).

[9] Possible boundary conditions are: (1) periodic boundary conditions, which imply that the spatial domain is a circle; (2) Dirichlet-type boundary conditions, which specify the concentration y on the boundary; and (3) Neumann-type boundary conditions, which specify the flux at the boundary. In one-dimensional domain $\mathcal{O} = [-L, L]$, these conditions imply for all t: (a) $y(t, -L) = y(t, L)$; (b) hostile boundaries $y(t, -L) = y(t, L) = 0$; and (c) zero flux at the boundaries or $\frac{\partial y(t,-L)}{\partial x} = \frac{\partial y(t,L)}{\partial x} = 0$.

[10] The evolution equations are shown in Appendix A.

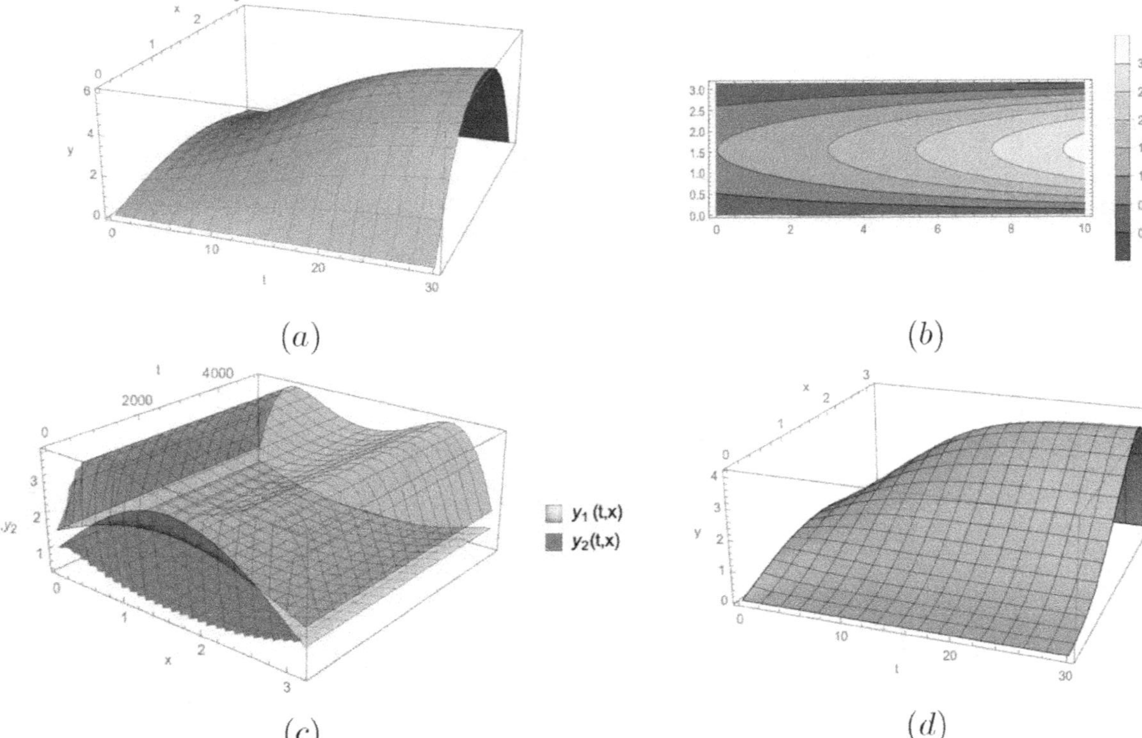

Figure 1   (a) Biomass evolution in time and space (t, x) of a population with logistic growth under linear diffusion. (b) Contours of the evolution surface. (c) Biomass evolution in time and space (t, x) of two interacting populations with logistic growth under linear diffusion (reaction-diffusion system). (d) Case (a) with advection.

When diffusivity D depends on the concentration or the spatial location, diffusion is nonlinear. Nonlinear diffusion in spatial models of climate change is modeled by the term $D\frac{\partial}{\partial x}\left[(1-x^2)\frac{\partial T(t,x)}{\partial x}\right]$, where $x \in [-1,1]$ is the sine of latitude and $T(t,x)$ is surface temperature at the latitude with sine x. More details will be presented in Section 6.2.4.

2.2 Long-Range Transport

Spatial diffusion captures local or short-range spatial interactions (Murray, 2003). In economics as well as in environmental and resource management, spatial interactions and spatial effects could be long range. This means that the rate of change of the concentration at a specific location x is affected by the concentrations of all other locations $x' \in \mathcal{O}$. These long-range interactions can be expressed by the model

$$\frac{\partial y(t,x)}{\partial t} = f(y(t,x), u(t,x), Y(t,x)), \; y(0,x) = y_0(x) \tag{2}$$

$$Y(t,x) = \mathbf{K}y(t,x) := \int_{\mathcal{O}} w(x-x')\, y(t,x')\, dx', \tag{3}$$

and appropriate boundary conditions. In (3), $\mathbf{K} = \int_{\mathcal{O}} w(x-x')\, dx'$ is a linear integral operator acting on a function $y(t,x)$ and $w(x-x')$ is a kernel function that models the effect that location x' has on location x.[11] Since one of the basic premises of spatial economics is that what happens near us matters more than what happens far from us, it is reasonable to assume that the kernel is declining with the distance $|x-x'|$, and that the influence tends to zero when this distance becomes sufficiently large. Another usual assumption is that the effects are spatially symmetric. Spatial kernels could reflect positive effects such as knowledge or productivity spillovers, or negative effects such as congestion effects. Kernels are usually modeled by exponential functions. Figure 2(a) depicts the spatiotemporal evolution of biomass under long-range effects.[12]

Figures 1 and 2 show[13] an interesting qualitative characteristic of the transport mechanisms in continuous time and space. In Figure 1 the spatial heterogeneity of the concentration is preserved with the passage of time, while in Figure 2(b) the initial spatial heterogeneity vanishes and the concentration

---

[11] Integrable kernel functions have been used in economics to model geographic spillovers (e.g., Krugman, 1996; Lucas, 2001; Lucas and Rossi-Hansberg, 2002; Chincarini and Asherie, 2008; Kyriakopoulou and Xepapadeas, 2013, 2017; Brock et al., 2014a, 2014d).

[12] The kernel and the evolution equation are shown in Appendix A.

[13] Predation is the functional response of a predator to a change in the density of the prey. The response could be unsaturated, depicted by a straight line from the origin in the space of prey-density predation, or saturated, depicted by concave or convex-concave functions bounded above in the same space (e.g., Murray, 2002).

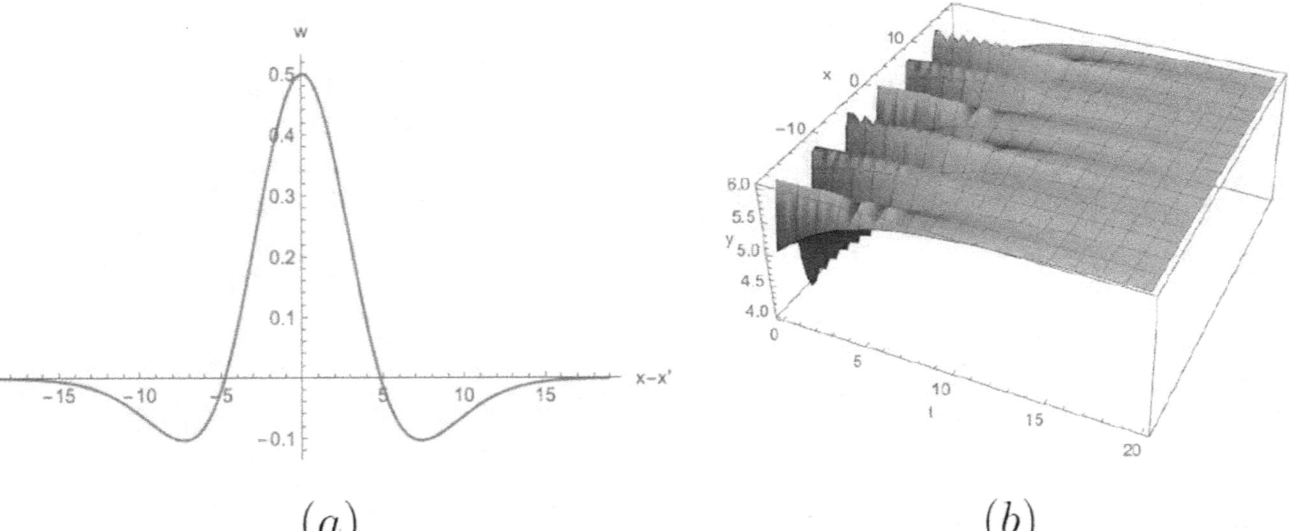

(a)

(b)

Figure 2 (a) Exponential kernel with positive and negative spatial effects. (b) Biomass evolution in time and space (t, x) of a population with logistic growth and nonlinear predation[13] effects under long-range transport.

becomes spatially homogeneous, or returns to a "flat earth" situation. The emergence of spatial heterogeneity – or spatial pattern formation – from an initial state of flat earth, or the convergence to flat from an initial state of spatial heterogeneity, is an important issue when the system is controlled optimally and is related to the design of efficient spatial policies. These issues are examined in Sections 4 and 4.1.

2.3 Discrete Space: Metapopulation Models and Dispersion

A class of spatial models – metapopulation models – most often encountered in environmental and resource economics treats space as discrete, consisting of patches, and describes how populations or other objects move across patches.[14] In bioeconomics based on metapopulation models, harvesting takes place in a patchy spatial domain and populations on different patches are connected by the dispersal process. Dispersion is modeled by a system of ODEs which, for a spatial domain with $i = 1,\ldots,n$ patches, can be written as

$$\frac{dy_i(t)}{dt} = f_i(y_i(t), u_i(t)) + \sum_{j=1, j \neq i}^{n} d_{ij} y_j(t) - D_i y_i(t),$$

$$y_i(0) = y_{i0}, \quad \sum_{j=1, j \neq i}^{n} d_{ij} \leq D_i, \tag{4}$$

where $f_i(y_i(t), u_i(t))$ represent population dynamics, and individuals disperse from patch i at a rate $D_i \geq 0$ and arrive from patch j at a rate $d_{ij} \geq 0$ (Cantrell and Cosner, 2003). Models like (4) can be extended to include density-dependent dispersal, multispecies interactions, bioinvasions, or pollution flows across patches. There is a considerable amount of literature that analyzes environmental and resource management issues using patchy environments and metapopulation models with dispersion across patches.[15]

Dispersion models have been used to study the "acid rain game" (e.g., Mäler, 1989; Kaitala et al., 1992; Mäler and de Zeeuw, 1998; Nagase and Silva, 2007) in which acid deposits damage regions due to acid rain generated by sulfur emissions in other regions. In Mäler and de Zeeuw (1998), acid depositions in each of the $i = 1,\ldots,n$ countries are given by Ae, where $A = [a_{ij}], i, j = 1,\ldots n$ is a transportation matrix in which the element a_{ij} denotes the fraction of country j's emissions e_j of sulfur or nitrogen oxides that is deposited in

---

[14] For the analysis of metapaulation models, see Levin (1974, 1976), Hastings (1982), and Hastings and Harrison (1994).

[15] See, for example, Wilen (2007) or Smith et al. (2009) and the references therein, and Section 5.1 for further analysis.

country i, so $A\mathbf{e}$ is the vector of acid depositions in each country. Acid deposition tions deplete each country's acid buffer stock if they exceed a critical load. The evolution of depletions is given by the system of ODEs

$$\dot{\mathbf{d}}(t) = A\mathbf{e}(t) - \mathbf{c}, \mathbf{d}(0) = \mathbf{d}_0,$$

where $\mathbf{d}$ is the vector of depletion of each country's acid buffer stock and $\mathbf{c}$ is the vector of critical loads. An increase in depletion means damage to the country's soil. The objective is to choose emission paths to minimize the cost of reducing emissions plus damages from depletion.

Metapopulation models have also been used in the study of biological invasions. Albers et al. (2010) study the spread of invasive species over heterogeneous regions and compare optimal spatially heterogeneous policy to spatially uniform policy. Epanchin-Nieli and Wilen (2012) study optimal spatial control of biological invasions in spatiotemporal models in which the spatial domain is two-dimensional. Bioinvasion spreads from the invaded cell to adjacent cells in the absence of regulation. Epanchin-Nieli and Wilen develop optimal policy with a spatially explicit characterization.

Brock and Xepapadeas (2002) analyze a species competition for a limited resource in a patchy environment. They show that three different equilibrium species specialization patterns emerge – undisturbed nature with harvesting, and private optimal and social optimal with harvesting – and show that policy rules are spatially dependent.

Dispersion type of modeling has been used to study heat transport from the equator to the North Pole in the economics of climate change. This includes "two-box" models in which heat moves from the equatorial region to the North and causes Arctic amplification.[16]

Spatial kernels can also be incorporated into spatial domains consisting of patches. In this case, (4) can be written as

$$\frac{dy_i(t)}{dt} = f\left(y_i(t), u_i(t), \sum_{j=1,\,j\neq i}^{n} w_{ij}y_j\right), \quad y_i(0) = y_{i0},$$

where the w_{ij} element of the kernel provides a measure of the influence of the state of the system at patch j on the state of the system at patch i.

Section 5 shows how the transport mechanisms presented in this section have been used to analyze specific issues in environmental and resource economics.

---

[16] See, for example, Alexeev et al. (2005), Alexeev and Jackson (2013), and Brock and Xepapadeas (2017, 2019, 2020).

3 Dynamic Optimization in Space-Time: A Spatial Maximum Principle under Diffusion and Long-Range Transport

In environmental and resource economics, transition dynamics modeled by (1), (2), or (4) are typically used as constraints in optimization problems in which the objective is to maximize the present discounted value of an objective depending on state y and control u, which are defined over the entire spatial domain. In the context of continuous time and space, this can be regarded as the problem of a social planner or environmental regulator defined as[17]

$$\max_{u \in \mathcal{U}} \int_{x \in \mathcal{O}} \int_0^\infty e^{-\rho t} U(y(t,x), u(t,x)) dt dx \tag{5}$$

subject to (1) or (2), where $U(\cdot, \cdot)$ is a standard utility or net benefit function and ρ is the utility discount rate. Problem (5) is not the typical dynamic optimization problem encountered in economics, since the constraints are either PDEs or IDEs.

Necessary optimality conditions can, however, be stated in terms of a spatial maximum principle that extends Pontryagin's maximum principle for optimal control in the temporal domain to a spatiotemporal domain,[18] as follows. If the path $u^*(t,x), y^*(t,x)$ solves problem (5) subject to (1), then there exists a costate $p(t,x)$ such that u^* maximizes the current value Hamiltonian function[19]

$$\mathcal{H}(y,p,u) = U(y,u) + p \left(f(y,u) + D \frac{\partial y^2}{\partial x^2} \right), \text{ or} \tag{6}$$

$$u^*(y,p) = \arg\max_u \mathcal{H}(y,p,u), \tag{7}$$

y^* and p satisfy the system of PDEs

$$\frac{\partial y^*}{\partial t} = f(y^*, u^*) + D \frac{\partial^2 y}{\partial x^2} \tag{8}$$

$$\frac{\partial p}{\partial t} = \rho p - \frac{\partial \mathcal{H}(y^*, p, u^*)}{\partial y} - D \frac{\partial^2 p}{\partial x^2}, \tag{9}$$

and a transversality condition at infinity is satisfied,

$$\lim_{t \to \infty} \int_{\mathcal{O}} e^{-\rho t} y^*(t,x) p(t,x) \, dx = 0. \tag{10}$$

---

[17] To simplify, we assume that transition dynamics are time autonomous and that the utility function $U(y,u)$ does not explicitly depend on time t.

[18] We present only the conditions here; for details and derivations see, for example, Derzko et al. (1984), Brock and Xepapadeas (2008), Brock et al. (2014b), and Xepapadeas and Yannacopoulos (2023).

[19] We drop (t,x) to ease notation.

Appendix B provides a sketch of a heuristic proof of result (8)–(9), and a solution procedure for this problem. Problems in finite terminal time can be handled by adding appropriate terminal and transversality conditions. Appendix C presents a method for solving a linear quadratic problem (see (14)–(15) below). It is important to note that in (9) diffusivity has a negative sign as opposed to the positive diffusivity of (8). Since y can be interpreted as quantity at spatial point x while p can be interpreted as the shadow value (i.e., price of a useful resource, or cost in the case of a pollutant) of this quantity at x, the opposite signs imply that quantities and prices move in opposite directions in the spatial domain.

With long-range spatial effects modeled by kernels, the extension of the maximum principle provides the following necessary conditions (Brock et al., 2014a, 2014d):

$$u^*(y,p) = \arg\max_u \mathcal{H}(y,p,u,Y) \tag{11}$$

$$\mathcal{H}(y,p,u) = U(y,u) + pf(y,u,Y),$$

where y^* and p satisfy the system of IDEs with appropriate spatial boundary conditions

$$\frac{\partial y^*}{\partial t} = f(y^*,u^*,Y^*)\ ,\ Y^* = \mathbf{K}y^*(t,x) \tag{12}$$

$$\frac{\partial p}{\partial t} = \rho p - \frac{\partial \mathcal{H}(y^*,p,u^*,Y^*)}{\partial y} - \mathbf{K}\frac{\partial \mathcal{H}(y^*,p,u^*,Y^*)}{\partial Y}, \tag{13}$$

along with the intertemporal transversality condition.

4 Spatial Pattern Formation

Patterns in space refer to spatial or spatiotemporal forms or regularities that are observable as different concentrations of a quantity of interest, such as biomass, pollutants, temperature, stock of capital or knowledge at different spatial points. If there is no spatial transport, the system will remain at its initial spatial state and no new patterns will emerge. A fundamental question in this context is whether spatial transport can create the endogenous emergence of patterns from a spatially homogeneous or flat-earth state. In biology the issue of pattern formation is referred to as morphogenesis and pattern formation mechanisms try to explain classic questions such as "how the leopard got its spots."

A fundamental pattern formation mechanism under spatial diffusion is the Turing mechanism (Turing, 1952). In general, a diffusion process in a system of interacting populations or materials tends to produce a spatially uniform population density, that is, spatial homogeneity. Thus it might be expected that diffusion acts as a homogenizing force or a stabilizer in case of spatial perturbations. There is however one exception, known as diffusion-induced instability or diffusive instability. Turing suggested that under certain conditions, diffusion acting on reaction-diffusion systems can generate spatially heterogeneous patterns.

This is the so-called Turing mechanism[20] for generating diffusion instability, often just called *Turing instability*, which means that a flat-earth state is destabilized by diffusion and this destabilization is a precursor to the emergence of persistent spatial patterns. The Turing mechanism requires a system of at least two interacting state variables, and its applications are not directly linked to explicit dynamic optimization. Thus a question that is relevant for environmental and resource economics is whether a system in which an environmental variable is transported across space through natural mechanisms, and a forward-looking agent – e.g., a regulator – is seeking to control the system optimally, can exhibit pattern formation in the space of quantities-shadow values. If the optimal control of a system with a diffusive externality like problem (5) generates an optimal spatial pattern, the important policy question then is what kind of policy can support this optimal spatial pattern.

Brock and Xepapadeas (2008) were the first to show that diffusion can destabilize a flat-earth steady state in the quantities-shadow values (state-costate) space, or equivalently in the state-control space, in a way that is similar to the Turing mechanism. The reasoning behind the optimal diffusion instability can be explained in the following way. From standard optimal control theory we know that, without diffusion (i.e., $D = 0$ in (1)) and under appropriate concavity assumptions, if a steady state defined as $(y^*, p^*) : (\dot{y} = 0, \dot{p} = 0)$ exists, then this steady state will have the local saddle point property or it will be unstable (e.g., Kurz, 1968).

The steady state with the saddle point property is spatially homogeneous, or a flat optimal steady state (FOSS). This means that a stable manifold exists – which is globally stable under appropriate assumptions – such that for any initial value for the state (e.g., stock of greenhouse gases, or biomass) there is an initial value for the costate (the shadow value of the externality) and the control, such that the system will stay on the stable manifold and converge to the FOSS. If a temporal perturbation moves the system away from the steady state but the system is optimally controlled, then on the stable manifold the perturbation will die out with the passage of time and the system will return to the FOSS.

---

[20] See also Levin and Segel (1985) and Murray (2003).

In the context of a flat-earth system without diffusion that evolves in time and space, a FOSS can be interpreted as a state $(y^*(x), p^*(x))$: $\left(\frac{\partial y(t,x)}{\partial t} = 0, \frac{\partial p(t,x)}{\partial t} = 0\right)$, with $(y^*(x), p^*(x)) = (y^*(x'), p^*(x'))$, for all x, $x' \in \mathcal{O}$. The stable manifold for this FOSS indicates that for any spatially homogeneous (flat) initial value for the state $y(0, x)$, there are flat initial values for the costate and the control such that the system will converge to the FOSS.

Suppose now that spatial diffusion occurs and that the FOSS is perturbed in the spatiotemporal domain. The optimality conditions from the extended Pontryagin's principle suggest that spatial sinusoidal wave-like patterns will emerge at the stable manifold in the neighborhood of the FOSS. If, with the passage of time, these patterns die out, then the FOSS is stable and the system will return to this FOSS. If, however, the patterns keep growing over time, then diffusion destabilizes the stable manifold in the neighborhood of the FOSS.

We call the emergence of spatial patterns in the optimally controlled system *optimal Turing instability*, which induces optimal spatial patterns. To obtain a better picture of optimal Turing instability, consider the linear quadratic optimal control problem

$$\max_{u(t,x)} \int_0^L \int_0^\infty e^{-\rho t}\left[-\frac{A}{2}y(t,x)^2 - \frac{B}{2}u(t,x)^2 + Ny(t,x)u(t,x)\right]dtdx \quad (14)$$

$$A, B, \rho > 0, \ AB - N^2 > 0$$

$$\text{s.t.} \ \frac{\partial y(t,x)}{\partial t} = Fy(t,x) - Gu(t,x) + D\frac{\partial^2 y(t,x)}{\partial x^2} \ F, G > 0, \quad (15)$$

with the solution analyzed in detail in Appendix C. Setting $\alpha \equiv \left(F - \frac{GN}{B}\right)$, $\beta \equiv \left(A - \frac{N^2}{B}\right)\left(\frac{G^2}{B}\right)$, we show in Appendix D (theorem 1) that optimal Turing instability will emerge for parameter values in the non-empty set

$$T \equiv R \cap S, \left\{(\alpha, \beta) : \alpha > \frac{\rho}{2}\right\} \cap \left\{(\alpha, \beta) : \beta < \frac{\rho^2}{4}\right\}.$$

The Turing set T for different values of the discount rate ρ is shown as the shaded areas of Figure 3. When the set is non-empty, then a $D > 0$ can be found that destabilizes the FOSS. The Turing set is empty for $\rho = 0$.

Since in a system with diffusive externality the costate is the price of the externality, this result suggests that due to diffusion the externality should be priced differently at different spatial points or, equivalently, the optimal control should be different at different locations. If the diffusive externality has

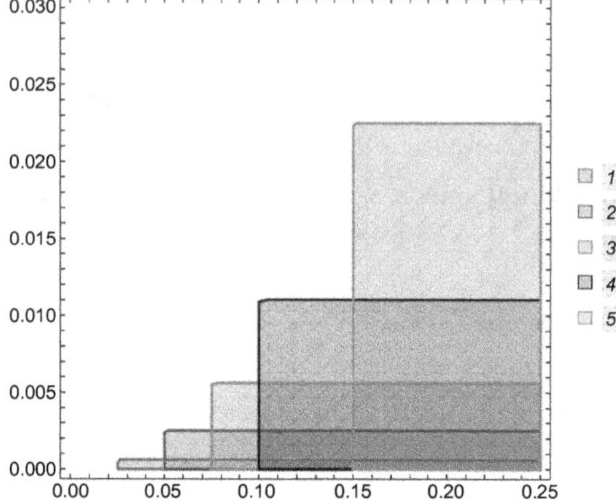

Legend: 1:$\rho = 0.05$; 2:$\rho = 0.1$; 3:$\rho = 0.15$; 4:$\rho = 0.2$; 5:$\rho = 0.3$
$\alpha \in [0, 0.25], \beta \in [0, 0.3]$

Figure 3 The Turing set for the optimal Turing instability for different values of ρ.

wider impacts such as productivity effects, then additional spatially dependent instruments might be required to support the optimal spatial pattern.

The optimal diffusive instability can be regarded as a precursor to the emergence of agglomerations and clustering in optimally controlled systems. Diffusion may, however, have stabilizing effects. Consider for example an optimal control problem such as (14), with a steady state (y^*, p^*) that is completely unstable for $D = 0$. Then, as shown in Appendix D, there exists a Turing space T for the parameters of the problem and a diffusivity $D > 0$ such that the optimized system will converge to a FOSS along a stable manifold. In terms of policy, this result suggests that allowing transport of the material or resource associated with the state variable in the case of a diffusive externality will make it possible to regulate with a spatially uniform policy instrument.

The analysis above focused on optimal Turing instability as a precursor to persistent spatial patterns under diffusion. A similar approach can be used to study pattern formation induced by long-range spatial effects represented by kernels. A FOSS with the saddle point property could be destabilized by spatiotemporal perturbations induced by a spatial kernel as defined in (3). Destabilization refers to the stable manifold associated with the FOSS (Brock et al., 2014a, 2014d).[21]

---

[21] See Appendix E for a sketch of the procedure.

4.1 Optimal Pattern Formation and Policy Implications

In the case of optimized systems, the important differences between the "optimal spatial instability" – whether it is diffusion-driven or kernel-driven – and the celebrated Turing instability, which explains pattern formation in biological and chemical systems, are that: (a) contrary to the spirit of the Turing model, here the instability is driven by optimizing behavior, so it is the outcome of forward-looking optimizing behavior by economic agents and not the result of reaction-diffusion in chemical or biological agents; (b) the spatial patterns do not emerge between two state variables that in general reflect quantities, but between a state variable and its shadow price, thus the spatial pattern occurs in the price-quantity space; and (c) contrary again to the Turing approach, there is no need to have two or more diffusing/interacting state variables to generate patterns, but only one diffusing state. Optimization induces diffusion to the price system (the costate) and the interaction of the price-quantity system generates patterns.

The optimal Turing instability is quashed when the discount rate ρ becomes zero (see Figure 3). This relation of the discount rate to Turing instability can be linked with general results from the turnpike literature and the role of the utility discount rate. In the classical turnpike theory of multisectoral capital theory (Cass and Shell, 1976; McKenzie, 1976), a discount rate close to zero is associated with unique steady-state equilibria and global asymptotic stability. When the discount rate is close to zero, the optimal Turing instability is expected to vanish as well. As indicated in Xepapadeas and Yannacopoulos (2023) – in the context of an optimal growth model with spatial capital flows – the optimal Turing instability emerges from comparing benefits from moving towards a flat-earth optimal steady state after a perturbation. In systems without spatial diffusion, moving toward the optimal steady after a perturbation reduces the value loss. In systems with spatial diffusion, if the discount rate is sufficiently high, the benefits from moving towards a flat-earth steady state after a perturbation could be negative. From the social planner's point of view, this can be interpreted as suggesting that it is preferable to let patterns emerge instead of controlling the system to the flat-earth optimal steady state. Thus the optimal Turing instability can be regarded as a new form of instability that may emerge if diffusion is present and the discount rate is sufficiently high. Low discount rates, on the other hand, induce positive benefits from moving towards the steady state and pattern elimination.[22] The role of the discount rate should

---

[22] Boucekkine et al. (2013) provide a similar pattern-eliminating low discount rate result for an *AK* model with linear diffusion. In this case, optimal patterns depend on the productivity parameter and the elasticity of marginal utility.

also be important in a potential integration of optimal Turing theory with Pareto optima in general equilibrium theory, which could be an area of future research to extend the work of Bewley (1982) in the integration of equilibrium theory and turnpike theory to spatial settings with diffusion.

Optimal spatial patterns or agglomeration as persistent outcomes implies that the value of the spatially heterogeneous system exceeds the value of the flat-earth system. In terms of policy design, an interesting distinction could be made between privately optimal solutions that ignore the diffusive or the long-range externality, and the socially optimal solution that internalizes the spatial externality. If spatial transport phenomena produce different outcomes between the social optimum and the private optimum – for example, if the equilibrium outcome at the private optimum implies spatial heterogeneity while the social optimum implies different spatial patterns or even flat earth – then policy instruments that promote socially optimal patterns or suppress spatial heterogeneity should be designed. In the remainder of this Element, we use the analytical tools presented earlier to study the issue of characterizing and designing policies under spatial transport for typical environmental and resource problems.

4.2 Cooperative and Noncooperative Solution Concepts in Continuous Space

Consider – at time t and location $x \in [0, L] = \mathcal{X}$ – a benefit function $B\left(u(t, x)\right)$, where $B(u)$ denotes gross benefits generated by a polluting activity u, with $B' \geq 0, B'' < 0, \lim_{u \to 0} B'(u) = \infty$, and $C(S)$ an increasing convex cost function of the accumulated pollution stock. Net benefits accrue to an economic agent located at x. Each agent is characterized by "spatial myopia," since the agent takes into account pollution costs associated with the stock of pollution accumulated only at its location and ignores the impact of its actions on the rest of the spatial domain. In contrast to each individual agent, a social planner that seeks to internalize the pollution externality would take into account the aggregate pollution costs associated with the stock of pollution accumulated in each location. Furthermore, pollution costs could exhibit spatial dependence emerging from the fact that damages at a location x do not depend on stock accumulation at x only but on accumulation in nearby locations x' as well, with the impact declining with distance. Using a kernel to capture proximity effects, the social damage function can be defined as

$$SD(t, x) = \int_{x \in \mathcal{X}} w(x - x')C(S(t, x')dx'.$$

A general spatiotemporal evolution of the pollution stock can be written as

$$\partial_t S(t,x) = u(x,t) + \int_{\mathcal{X}\setminus x} \phi(x-x')u(t,x')dx' - bS(t,x) + D\partial_{xx}S(t,x).$$

$$(16)$$

The integral term in (16) reflects long-range effects of emissions generated at x' by agents other than the agent located at x, in addition to the local diffusion effects of the stock on location x.

Interpreting S as the local abundance of a renewable resource, introducing a local growth function $F(S(t,x))$, and interpreting $u(t,x)$ as local harvesting, the dynamics of (16) describe the spatiotemporal evolution of a renewable resource. In this case, the integral term represents harvesting in x of harvesters located in x', if this is possible under the property rights structure (e.g., open access).

A cooperative solution is the solution to the following social planner's problem:

$$\max_{\{u(t,x)\}} J = \max_{\{u(t,x)\}} \int_0^\infty e^{-\rho t} \int_{\mathcal{X}} [B(u(t,x)) - SD(t,x)]\,dxdt,$$

subject to (16) with appropriate initial, boundary, and transversality conditions. In the renewable resource version of the same problem, $B(u)$ could be interpreted as net harvesting benefits and SD as additional benefits (existence values) or costs (stock effects) from the resource stock.

Noncooperative solutions can be associated with extensions of open-loop Nash equilibrium (OLNE) and feedback Nash equilibrium (FBNE) solution concepts. In OLNE, each agent follows a spatially myopic strategy, takes the actions of all other agents located at $x' \in \mathcal{X} \setminus x$ as exogenous (i.e., $u(t,x)$), and commits to an emission path that optimizes its own objective. That is,

$$\max_{\{u(t,x)\}} J^O = \max_{\{u(t,x)\}} \int_0^\infty e^{-\rho t} [B(u(t,x)) - SD(t,x)]\,dxdt,$$

subject to

$$\partial_t S(t,x) = u(x,t) + \int_{\mathcal{X}\setminus x} \phi(x-x')\bar{u}(t,x')dx' - bS(t,x) + D\partial_{xx}S(t,x). \quad (17)$$

In FBNE, each agent does not recall the previous history of the system, as described by past values of the state $S(t,x)$, and assumes that the other agents' emissions are conditioned on the current pollution accumulation in the spatial domain. There are different ways to interpret the relationship between agents' emissions and the accumulated pollutant, which describes the equilibrium feedback strategy. One way is to assume that $u(t,x) = \theta\left(\int_{\mathcal{X}} S(t,x)dx, x\right)$ so all agents condition their emissions on the aggregate current stock. Another way is to assume that $u(t,x) = \theta\left(\int_{\mathcal{X}} \phi(x-x')S(t,x')\right)dx'$, with $\phi(0) = 1$. This means that each agent conditions emissions on the pollution stock accumulated at its location. The optimization problem, for the case of FBNE, can be written as:

$$\max_{\{u(t,x)\}} J^{\mathrm{F}} = \max_{\{u(t,x)\}} \int_0^\infty e^{-\rho t} \left[B\left(u(t,x)\right) - SD(t,x) \right] dxdt,$$

subject to

$$\partial_t S(t,x) = u(x,t) + \int_{\mathcal{X} \setminus x} \theta \left(\int_{\mathcal{X}} S(t,x)dx, x \right) dx' - bS(t,x) + D\partial_{xx}S(t,x), \quad (18)$$

with the θ function representing the equilibrium feedback strategy.

Cooperative and OLNE problems can be solved using the extension of the Pontryagin's principle presented in Section 3 (e.g., Xepapadeas, 2022). For the solution of FBNE problems, the use of the maximum principle encounters difficulties since the the equilibrium feedback strategy θ is not known a priori and should be determined endogenously. In this case, the dynamic programming approach is used in a similar way to how it is used for the analysis of the temporal only FBNE problems. The full solution of these problems, including potentially nonlinear feedbacks in dynamics, nonlinearities in diffusion, and long-range effects, is a very interesting area for further research. A starting point could be the solution of the Hamilton-Jacobi-Bellman (HJB) equation in infinite dimensional Hilbert space following the approach of Boucekkine et al. (2013) for a problem without strategic interactions, in which the solution for an isoelastic utility function is obtained by looking for solutions for the HJB with an isoelastic value function. A feedback solution to a spatial differential game with linear diffusion and isoelastic objective is provided by de Frutos et al. (2021) by considering affine functions as a solution for the infinite-dimensional HJB equation. Boucekkine et al. (2022b) in a similar context show that there exists a Markov perfect equilibrium, unique among the class of the affine feedbacks.

PART II APPLICATIONS

5 Environmental and Resource Management Policy under Spatial Dynamics

The spatial characteristics of environmental policy emerge naturally when there is spatial differentiation with respect to a specific characteristic (e.g., land quality) or a flow of a pollutant or biomass across regions or spatial locations, which is often referred to as cross-border or transboundary. When pollution – that is, the externality – crosses borders,[23] there are two major types of issues related to policy design. The first type is the case in which pollution is a local "public bad" or, to put it differently, environmental quality is a local public good. This means that damages emerge from the local pollution level after local emissions and spatial dispersion of pollutants takes place. In this case, environmental policy has to correct the local externality. A typical example is upstream-downstream water pollution problems. The second type is the case of a global externality, or global public bad, in which damages in each region are associated with global pollution and are independent of the spatial point from which pollution originates. A typical example is the case of climate change.

The flow of the pollutants or the resources implies the existence of a transport mechanism such as the one described in Section 2, which provides the link between the forward-looking optimization of economics and the natural laws governing the flow of pollutants or resources. We focus on this link as the driver of spatiotemporal patterns and location-specific policies, which can internalize externalities, including spatial externalities.

The largest part of the existing literature on pollution control or bioeconomic analysis that considers space focuses on discrete space, often with a temporal dimension that is either dynamic or fixed. However, aside from some notable exceptions in the literature related to fishery management – and, to a lesser extent, the literature regarding groundwater management, pollution control, bioinvasions, or acid rain issues – the main body of the environmental and resource management literature does not include explicit spatial transport mechanisms across locations.

An important strand of literature, developed mainly in the 1990s, studies the link between environmental quality and international trade. Two seminal papers by Copeland and Taylor (1994, 1995) analyze pollution and trade. In the first, pollution does not disperse across countries. In this case, free trade shifts pollution-intensive production to the country where human capital is scarce, and world pollution increases. In the second, pollution crosses boundaries and is a global public bad such as climate change or ozone depletion. One of the results is that if countries are different, trade creates "pollution havens," which are countries in which pollution-intensive industries locate due to lax environmental policies. This result suggests that under global pollution, spatial patterns related to the pollution intensity of production emerge.

---

[23] The borders could refer to nations or to subnational jurisdictions.

Spatial patterns are induced by international trade. In the same analytical framework, Silva and Caplan (1997) study environmental policy for a global public bad in the context of a federal system. Copeland (1996), in a two-country static model with unidirectional cross-border pollution and international trade,[24] derives optimal tariff policy for a country that imports goods and is harmed by cross-border pollution generated in the neighboring country, while Hatzipanayotou et al. (2002, 2005) study multilateral policy reforms under cross-border pollution, international trade, and foreign aid.[25]

There is extensive literature on dynamic models of global pollution that is accumulated in the ambient environment. The growth of global pollutants depends on aggregate emissions per unit time originating from different agents. In these models, the spatial dimension is implicit, since it is natural to assume that agents emit from different spatial locations. However, since there is no transport mechanism, it is difficult to value the spillover externality. The analysis of these problems focuses on two types of solution concepts: a cooperative solution, in which a regulator maximizes aggregate welfare net of damages; and noncooperative solutions, in which each location is treated as a forward-looking agent that maximizes own welfare net of own damages by taking into account the behavior of the other forward-looking agents. Two types of behavior are in general examined: the OLNE in which each agent takes the emission paths of the other agents as given, and the FBNE in which the emissions of each agent depend on the current stock of pollution accumulation (Başar and Olsder, 1995). The feedback solution is Markov perfect by construction. Typical examples of this modeling are the cases of transboundary pollution games (e.g., Van der Ploeg and de Zeeuw, 1992; Dockner and Long, 1993)[26] and the lake games (e.g., Brock and Starrett, 2003; Mäler et al., 2003; Wagener, 2003; Kossioris et al., 2008, 2011).

This discussion suggests that the spatial dimension is implicit in a large number of issues that are central to environmental and resource economics. However, the absence of explicit transport mechanisms, such as those reviewed in previous sections, does not allow for full exploration of the impact of spatial dynamics on environmental and resource management. In this section, we present specific applications in spatially structured environments in which flows are explicitly driven by spatial transport mechanisms. Our aim is to show how this

---

[24] Pollution flows in a two-region model is a special case of the general dispersion model (4) with $i = 2$. Unidirectional flows, for example, means that $d_{12} = D$ and $d_{21} = 0$. For transboundary pollution flows and the emergence of regional inequalities see Levin and Xepapadeas (2017).

[25] For a survey on environmental policy and international trade, see Ulph (1997).

[26] For surveys, see, for example, Jorgensen et al. (2010) and Calvo and Rubio (2012).

analytical framework could be helpful in better understanding spatial heterogeneity and spatial patterns as outcomes of optimizing behavior, and also in the design of efficient space-dependent policies.

5.1 Fishery Management in Patchy Environments

In fishery management, the explicit introduction of space is implemented in the context of metapopulation models with subpopulations in patches and population dispersal among them due to natural forces (e.g., winds or currents).

Smith et al. (2009) present spatial dynamic processes and their applications to renewable resource management. Sanchirico and Wilen (1999) use the modeling approach in (4) to describe the evolution of fish biomass in patch $i = 1, \ldots, n$ under harvesting modeled by the catch function $h_i \left(E_i \left(t \right), y_i \left(t \right) \right)$, with $E_i \left(t \right)$ being the level of fishing effort. In an open-access patchy system, fishing effort and biomass in each patch could evolve as

$$\frac{dE_i \left(t \right)}{dt} = s_i R_i \left(y_i \left(t \right), E_i \left(t \right) \right)$$

$$+ \sum_{j=1, j \neq i}^{n} s_{ij} \left[R_i \left(y_i \left(t \right), E_i \left(t \right) \right) - R_j \left(y_j \left(t \right), E_j \left(t \right) \right) \right]$$

$$\frac{dy_i \left(t \right)}{dt} = f_i \left(y_i \left(t \right) \right) y_i \left(t \right) + ND_i \left(y_1 \left(t \right), \ldots, y_n \left(t \right) \right) - h_i \left(E_i \left(t \right), y_i \left(t \right) \right),$$

where $f_i \left(y_i \right)$ is per capita growth function; ND_i is the net dispersal function in patch i; $R_i \left(y_i, E_i \right)$ denotes rents in patch i; s_i is entry exit rates; and $s_{ij} \left(R_i \left(y_i, E_i \right) - R_j \left(y_j, E_j \right) \right)$ is fleet dispersal because of revenue differentials across patches. The biomass-effort steady state of the system is determined as $\left(E_i^*, y_i^* \right) : \left(dE_i / dt = 0, dy_i / dt = 0 \right)$. Sanchirico and Wilen find the equilibrium patterns of biomass and effort across the system to be dependent upon bioeconomic conditions within each patch, and the nature of the biological dispersal mechanism between patches. In terms of policy, they conclude that optimal instruments should reflect the interplay between the spatial gradient of rents and the spatial gradient of biological dispersal.

Sanchirico and Wilen (2001) study the creation of marine reserves in a patchy environment and show that, under certain conditions, creating a reserve by closing a patch for harvesting could increase aggregate biomass and harvest.[27]

---

[27] For further analysis of bioeconomic models in patchy environments and issues related to marine reserves, see, for example, Smith and Wilen (2003), Costello and Polasky (2004, 2008), Sanchirico and Wilen (2005), and Smith et al. (2009).

Rassweiler et al. (2012) studied optimal fishery management and marine protected areas in a patchy environment. In this model, annual yield Y_{it} in patch i and year t is given by

$$Y_{it} = \frac{B_{Lit} E_{it} \left(1 - e^{-(E_{it}+M)}\right)}{E_{it} + M},$$

where B_{Lit}, E_{it}, M are legal-sized fish biomass, harvesting effort, and natural mortality rate, respectively. Profit in each patch per year is

$$\pi_{it} = Y_{it} - \theta_i E_{it},$$

where θ_i is cost per unit effort in patch i. The objective is to choose how to distribute total fishing effort among patches to maximize profits. It is shown that fully optimized spatial management could increase nearshore fishery profits relative to those obtained with nonspatial management, with the magnitude of these increases varying across species.[28]

In a continuous-space fishery model, Behringer and Upmann (2014) find that in atomistic equilibrium, each agent exploits one location only and tends to harvest the resource to extinction in this location. This result also points to spatially structured policy interventions. Reaction-diffusion processes have also been used to model fishery management in a continuous spatial domain. Broadbridge and Hutchinson (2022) develop such a model in a heterogeneous environment with spatially dependent diffusivity, while Cui et al. (2017) use reaction-diffusion modeling to study harvesting quotas and protection zones in fishery management.

5.2 Groundwater Management

In groundwater management, the early literature such as Gisser and Sanchez (1980), Negri (1989), and Provencher and Burt (1993) considered the underground aquifer as a homogeneous single-cell "bathtub" in which abstraction by one user caused an instantaneous impact on others. More recent literature recognizes the fact that hydrological factors such as seepage or aquifer transmissivity introduce a spatial pumping externality. In this case, pumping by a farmer affects and is affected by the pumping behavior of neighboring farmers through the emergence of overlapping cones of depression in the aquifer.

---

[28] Voss et al. (2018) also study the problem of evaluating economic and conservation benefits from spatially explicit fisheries management in patchy environments when there is a mismatch because ecological spatial structures are not reflected in how catch limits are set. They link gains from spatially dependent management with recruitment behavior when there is spatial heterogeneity in biological parameters.

Thus optimization problems which seek to maximize benefits from the underground aquifer acquire an explicit spatial structure (e.g., Saak and Peterson, 2007; Brozović et al., 2010).

Pfeiffer and Lin (2012) model a "patchy" groundwater aquifer with water flowing across patches according to hydrological rules. The dynamics of water stock $y_i(t)$ in each patch are given by

$$\frac{dy_i(t)}{dt} = -u_i(t) + g_i(u_i) + \sum_{j=1, j \neq i}^{n} \theta_{ij} y_j(t), \tag{19}$$

where u_i is water pumping, $g_i(u_i)$ is recharge to patch i, and flow parameters θ_{ij} are determined by Darcy's law or $\theta_{ij} = (y_i - y_j)/x_{ij}$, where x_{ij} is the distance between patches. Groundwater dynamics (19) act as a constraint to the problem of a social planner seeking to maximize discounted aquifer benefits, or

$$\max_{u_i(t)} \int_0^\infty e^{-\rho t} \left[\sum_{i=1}^{n} [R_i(u_i) - C(y_i) u_i] \right] dt.$$

Results suggest that the spatial externality results in overpumping relative to the social optimum (Pfeiffer and Lin, 2012), and that the spatial externality is important for large, unconfined groundwater aquifers (e.g., Brozović et al., 2010). Kuwayama and Brozović (2013) consider the adoption of a spatially differentiated groundwater permit system to efficiently regulate when groundwater pumping affects the flow of surface water.

Brock and Xepapadeas (2010) studied a semiarid system with reaction-diffusion characteristics in which plant biomass and soil water interact and diffuse in a continuous space with linear (Fickian) diffusion. The plant–soil water dynamics are given by

$$\partial_t P(t, x) = g(W(t, x), P(t, x)) - bP(t, x) - h(t, x) + D_p \partial_{xx} P(t, x)$$
$$\partial_t W(t, x) = f(P(t, x), R) - v(W(t, x), P(t, x)) - r_W W(t, x)$$
$$+ D_w \partial_{xx} W(t, x) \, P(0, x), W(0, x) \, given,$$
$$P(t, 0) = P(t, L), W(t, 0) = W(t, L) \, \forall t,$$

where $P(t, x)$ is plant density (biomass); $W(t, x)$ is soil water at time $t \in [0, \infty)$ and location $x \in [0, L]$; R is fixed rainfall; h is harvesting of plant biomass through grazing; $g(W, P)$ is plant growth, increasing in soil water and plant density; bP is plant senescence; $f(P, R)$ is water infiltration; $v(W, P)$ is water uptake by plants; r_W is specific rate of water loss due to evaporation and percolation; and D_P and D_W are diffusion coefficients for plant biomass (plant dispersal) and soil water, respectively.[29] The authors consider the problem of a myopic agent that optimizes profits by ignoring spatiotemporal dynamics, and the problem of a social planner that internalizes the spatial externality. They find that at the myopic solution, spatial patterns in plant–soil water are generated through the Turing mechanism but the socially optimal solution is spatially homogeneous. Spatially dependent instruments are required in order to internalize the spatial externality.[30]

5.3 Pollution Control

Goetz and Zilberman (2000) consider pollution accumulation in a lake associated with the runoff from mineral fertilizers and animal manure. They employ a two-stage optimization, optimizing first across the spatial and then across the temporal dimension. The social optimum can be implemented with site-specific taxes on mineral fertilizers, manure, and large animal units.

Sigman (2005) considers transboundary river pollution and examines whether US states that, under decentralized policies, control their Clean Water Act programs free ride on downstream states. Sigman does not include an explicit pollution transport mechanism along the river and defines water quality WQ_{it} in location i and time t as

$$WQ_{it} = \sum_{h=1}^{H} \frac{P_{ht}}{F_{ht}} \delta^{h-i},$$

where P_{ht} is pollution at upstream locations h, F_{ht} is flow that dilutes pollution, and $\delta < 1$ is a spatial discount term that diminishes pollution effects with distance. Using econometric estimation, Sigman concludes that there is free riding, whose costs need, however, to be compensated with benefits derived from the flexibility introduced by decentralization.

Xabadia et al. (2006, 2008) study policies for controlling agricultural stock pollution in a framework in which the spatial differentiation is related to the heterogeneity in the land quality of producers located at different sites. Pollution generated by the heterogeneous producers is accumulated in the environment and the optimal emission policy is site specific. Although there is no explicit spatial transport mechanism, this research studies a spatially distributed parameter problem in the space of qualities which are distributed in space and presents another approach to spatial issues.

---

[29] We use ∂_z instead of $\partial/\partial x$ and similar notation for second derivatives to simplify.

[30] For a detailed numerical analysis of optimal harvesting in the semiarid system, see Uecker (2016). For the application of this methodology to invasive species control, see Liu and Sims (2016).

Explicit pollution diffusion across space was introduced by Brock and Xepapadeas (2008) into the so-called shallow-lake problem. In this case, pollution (phosphorous) accumulates in time and space according to the PDE

$$\partial_t P(t,x) = E(t,x) - mP(t,x) + f(P(t,x)) + D\partial_{xx}P(t,x), \tag{20}$$

with appropriate initial and spatial boundary conditions. In this setup, $P(t,x)$ denotes the stock of the pollutant at t and x; E is emissions by location x; m is the pollution decay rate; and $f(P(t,x))$ is in general a convex-concave function indicating nonlinear feedbacks that underlie the lake dynamics. Using (20) as a constraint in the planner's problem for maximizing benefits over the whole spatial domain, and realistic parametrization for the lake, it is shown that a steady state can be destabilized in the context of optimal Turing instability, and spatial patterns in the accumulation of the pollutant start emerging due to pollution diffusion. Since the spatial patterns for the pollutant imply spatial patterns for its shadow cost, this result suggests spatially differentiated emissions taxes.[31]

Camacho and Pérez-Barahona (2015) use the model of Gaussian plume to describe the spatial dynamics of pollution. They consider a pollution accumulation equation at location x of the form

$$\partial_t P(t,x) = E(x,t) + \partial_{xx}P(t,x)$$

in a model of optimal land use in which the interaction between land use and the environment generates a spatially heterogeneous solution and abatement technology is central in pollution stabilization. Cornet and Camacho (2021) study soil pollution diffusion in an agricultural economy model. In this model, output is produced by fertile and polluted land with given technology, and pollution diffuses in space with a constant diffusion coefficient as in (20). They provide conditions for pattern formation between fertile and polluted land.

De Frutos and Martín-Herrán (2019) consider a spatiotemporal pollution dynamics problem of the form shown in (20) without the nonlinear feedback to study optimal regulation in a transboundary pollution problem. By making a linear quadratic approximation and discretizing the space, they derive regional cooperative and noncooperative emission paths.

5.4 Urban Economics and Spatial Effects

Environmental externalities are prominent in the area of urban economics. Pollution from transportation or industrial activities affects the location decisions of both individuals and firms and significantly affects the spatial structure

---

[31] For a detailed numerical analysis of this problem, see Grass and Uecker (2017).

of a city. In this context, environmental policy is an important factor in the development of residential and industrial clusters, since strict environmental measures can discourage firms from polluting urban areas, while reduced pollution levels can encourage people to locate closer to industrial areas, thus reducing commuting costs.

Henderson (1977) studied a problem in which industrial pollution diffuses towards the residential/central business district boundary. The optimal policy consists of Pigouvian taxes along with regulations controlling the allocation of land between polluting firms and individuals, and potential redistribution of tax receipts between heavily taxed and lightly taxed communities. The combination of optimal taxes with zoning policies prevents polluting firms from locating in residential areas. Verhoef and Nijkamp (2002, 2005) use a monocentric city model and study first- and second-best policies in order to control the effect of industrial pollution on residential areas. They show that environmental goals can be promoted either at the expense of or in favor of agglomeration economies.

Arnott et al. (2008) study a circular city in which firms generate pollution and households commute at a cost and receive disutility from pollution. Pollution disperses according to a function $D(e(x), x - x')$, where $e(x)$ denotes emissions at x and $x - x'$ is the distance between location x and x'. The kernels introduced in Section 2.2 could be a reasonable specification of such a function. In this setup, the optimal allocation can be decentralized by imposing a tax per unit of area of industrial land at a particular location equal to the total damage caused by the pollution from that unit area, evaluated at the optimum. Location-specific Pigouvian taxes that do not fully internalize the total damage caused by this site are inefficient.

Rossi-Hansberg et al. (2010) and Rossi-Hansberg and Sarte (2012) study housing externalities, defined as the effects that a house's characteristics have on neighbors. They find that these externalities decay fast with distance, with the impact on location x from housing services $H(x')$ in nearby location $x' \in [-L, L]$ defined as:

$$\delta \int_{-L}^{L} e^{-\delta|x-x'|} H(x') \, dx'.$$

They conclude that the number of residents in a neighborhood depends on the quality of nearby housing and propose, as policy measures, minimum maintenance requirements or zoning policies.

Kyriakopoulou and Xepapadeas (2013, 2017) consider a linear city with: (i) productivity spillovers that decline with distance, or

$$z(x) = \delta \int_0^L e^{-\delta(x-x')^2} \lambda(x') \ln L(x') \, dx',$$

where $e^{-\delta(x-x')^2}$ is a normal dispersal kernel, $\lambda(x')$ is the proportion of land occupied by firms at the spatial point x', and $L(x')$ is labor input; and (ii) pollution, P, that diffuses across the city and concentrates in specific locations according to

$$\ln P(x) = \int_0^L e^{-\zeta(x-x')^2} \lambda(x') \ln E(x') \, dx',$$

where $E(x')$ denotes industrial pollution. In this setup, equilibrium and optimal solutions regarding the spatial structure of the city are compared and optimal policy is derived. In Kyriakopoulou and Xepapadeas (2013), where a first-nature advantage assumption is made, it is shown that the equilibrium outcome leads to either a monocentric city or a polycentric city with the first-nature advantage site attracting the majority of economic activity. On the contrary, the socially optimal solution leads to a duocentric city, where neither of the two centers is formed around the natural advantage site. The authors show that sites with inherent advantages can lose their comparative advantage when the social cost of pollution is taken into account.

Kyriakopoulou and Xepapadeas (2017) consider a general equilibrium setup where there is: competition for land between industries and households, polluting industrial activity, production externalities, and costly commuting. In equilibrium, the center of the city is mixed residential/industrial, while at the social optimum there are distinct residential and industrial clusters across the city. The presence of spatial productivity spillovers and spatial pollution spillovers requires that the optimal policy be site-specific and consist of two instruments: pollution taxes to internalize the negative pollution externality and labor subsidies to internalize the productivity externality. Uniform instruments are suboptimal.

Regnier and Legras (2018) use a model à la Fujita and Ogawa (1982) to study the urban patterns derived in the presence of industrial pollution, which decreases environmental quality E at spatial point x according to

$$E(x) = \bar{E} - \int_X [e - \eta |x - y|] b(y) \, dy,$$

where $\bar{E}$ denotes environmental quality without pollution, e is the quantity of pollution emitted by one firm, η shows how pollution disperses in space, $x - y$ is the distance between firm and household, and $b(y)$ is the density of firms at y. The authors show that the internalization of pollution forms more specialized areas in the city, which results in lower greenhouse gases from commuting.

There is also a growing literature on the internal structure of cities when pollution comes from commuting. Verhoef and Nijkamp (2003) point out the importance of space in the analysis of urban air pollution, which is affected by aggregate commuting and not by the number of commuters. Schindler et al. (2017) study how traffic-induced pollution affects residential choices and find that higher pollution levels reduce the size and the population of the city. Pollution (P), in that framework, increases with the traffic volume passing by r, as

$$P(r) = 1 + a + b \int_r^{r_f} n(r)dr,$$

where a and b measure the impacts of regional and traffic-induced pollution in the city and $n(r)$ is the number of people crossing location r. Finally, Denant-Boemont et al. (2018) show that polycentric cities imply higher welfare and lower pollution levels.

5.5 Pollution Diffusion and Growth

Spatial considerations in growth models associated with diffusion of capital in a spatial domain have been explored in the context of spatial growth theory. Spatial diffusion of capital and pollution, which is jointly generated by output production, is still an area that is not very well researched. La Torre et al. (2015) develop Solow- and Ramsey-type models with capital and pollution diffusion and concave or convex-concave production function. The process of capital and pollution accumulation is described for the augmented Solow model in a domain $[x_0, x_1]$ by the system

$$\partial_t k(t,x) = \frac{s(x)f\,(k(t,x)\,[1 - \tau(x)]}{\alpha + \beta P(t,x)^2} - \delta_k k(t,x) + D_k \partial_{xx} k(t,x)$$

$$\partial_t P(t,x) = \theta \int_{x_0}^{x_1} [1 - u(x')]\,f\,(k(t,x'))\,\phi(x',x)dx'$$

$$- \delta_P P(t,x) + D_P \partial_{xx} P(t,x),$$

where $k(x,t), P(t,x)$ denote capital stock and pollution at time t and location x, respectively, which depreciate at rates δ_k, δ_P; $f(\cdot)$ is a production function; $s(x)$, $\tau(x)$ denote saving rate and taxation at location x; $\alpha + \beta P(x,t)^2$ stands for output-reducing pollution-damage function; $u(x')$ denotes pollution reduction due to abatement at location x'; $\phi(x',x)$ is a kernel indicating the impact of pollution at x' on neighboring areas, and D_k, D_P are diffusion coefficients for capital and pollution respectively. Results obtained from numerical simulation suggest the emergence of a spatially heterogeneous distribution for the capital stock and pollution at a terminal time. The convex-concave production function indicates, under certain conditions, the possibility of elimination of poverty traps.

La Torre et al. (2021) study a transboundary pollution problem with pollution diffusion across space[32] and explore local solutions corresponding to decentralized outcomes in which local planners ignore the transboundary externality and global outcomes in which a social planner takes this externality into account. By comparing solutions, environmental taxes are characterized which are explicitly spatially heterogeneous when spatial heterogeneity exists in the initial pollution distributions.

5.6 Infectious Diseases and the Spatial Dimension

Traditional mathematical models describing the spread of infectious diseases (e.g., Hethcote, 1989, 2000) do not include the spatial dimension. Typically these models link flows between the passively immune class M, the susceptible class S, the exposed class E, the infective class I, and the recovered class R, with the passively immune class M and the latent period class E often being omitted because they are not crucial for the susceptible–infective interaction. If recovery does not provide immunity, then the model is called a susceptible–infective–susceptible (SIS) model, since individuals move from the susceptible class to the infective class and then back to the susceptible class upon recovery, while if individuals recover with permanent immunity, then the model is a susceptible–infective–recovered (SIR) model. Most of these models do not consider spatial diffusion of different classes in a given spatial domain, and analyze convergence of the classes to a spatially homogeneous steady state.

A simple model for the spatial spread of an epidemic (Murray, 2002, chapter 10) can be developed by augmenting a standard SIS model with diffusion terms describing the spread of susceptives and infectives on a one-dimensional space with fixed population, or

$$\partial_t S(t, x) = -\beta I(t, x) S(t, x) + D \partial_{xx} S(t, x) \tag{21}$$

$$\partial_t I(t, x) = \beta I(t, x) S(t, x) - \gamma I(t, x) + D \partial_{xx} I(t, x), \tag{22}$$

where $I(t, x), S(t, x)$ are infective and susceptive, respectively, at time t and location x, infectives have a disease-induced mortality rate γI, D is the diffusion coefficient, and β is a fixed parameter. Murray shows that this model generates a traveling epidemic wave of constant shape.

The spatial dimension can also be introduced using the concept of kernels introduced in Section 2.2. Consider an SIR model with $S + I + R$ fixed and independent of time t, evolving in a one-dimensional spatial domain. Following Ruan (2007) in the description of the Kendall model,[33] the rate of infection is assumed to be

$$\beta \int_{-\infty}^{\infty} I(t, y)K(x - y)dy,$$

where $\beta > 0$ is a fixed parameter and the kernel $K(x - y)$ describes the impact of infected individuals at location y on the infection of susceptible individuals at location x, under the assumption that $\int_{-\infty}^{\infty} K(y)dy = 1$. Then the SIR model becomes

$$\partial_t S(t, x) = -\beta S(t, x) \int_{-\infty}^{\infty} I(t, y)K(x - y)dy$$

$$\partial_t I(t, x) = \beta S(t, x) \int_{-\infty}^{\infty} I(t, y)K(x - y)dy - \gamma I(t, x)$$

$$\partial_t R(t, x) = \gamma I(t, x).$$

It can be shown that an initial infection does not propagate if $\gamma/\beta\sigma \geq 1$, where σ is the initial density of susceptibles. An SIR model that combines the kernel and diffusion characteristics with constant population[34] can be written as

$$\partial_t S(t, x) = -\beta S(t, x) \int_{-\infty}^{\infty} I(t, y)K(x - y)dy + D\partial_{xx} S(t, x)$$

$$\partial_t I(t, x) = \beta S(t, x) \int_{-\infty}^{\infty} I(t, y)K(x - y)dy - \gamma I(t, x) + D\partial_{xx} I(t, x)$$

$$\partial_t R(t, x) = \gamma I(t, x) + D\partial_{xx} R(t, x).$$

Belik et al. (2011) analyze the spatial spread of an epidemic in the context of a metapopulation reaction-diffusion system. Using an SIS model, the system becomes

$$\partial_t S_n(t) = -\beta \frac{I_n(t)S_n(t)}{N_n^s} + \sum_m (w_{nm} S_m - w_{mn} S_n) \tag{23}$$

$$\partial_t I_n(t) = \beta \frac{I_n(t)S_n(t)}{N_n^s} - \gamma I_n(t) + \sum_m (w_{nm} I_m - w_{mn} I_n), \tag{24}$$

where w_{nm} is dispersal from population at location m to n, and N_n^s is the number of individuals in population n in diffusive equilibrium.

---

[33] Kendall (1957, 1965) studied the spread of infectious diseases to a spatially extended population using a space-dependent integrodifferential equation.

[34] For more details of these models, see, for example, Lin et al. (2003), Ruan (2007), and La Torre et al. (2022).

A common characteristic of these models is that they do not involve any optimization and the main objective is to characterize the solution of the dynamical system given initial and boundary conditions and parameter values. These models acquire economic characteristics if an objective to be optimized is introduced and the dynamical system acts as a constraint set to the optimization problem. La Torre (2024) develop an SIS epidemic-economic model with spatial diffusion for the susceptibles and infectives as in (21)–(22) for COVID control.[35] The objective is to choose optimal lockdown policies that limit social interactions to minimize aggregate costs consisting of lost output due to lockdown measures and disease prevalence.

Ferraccioli et al. (2024) develop a spatiotemporal model with heterogeneous mixed populations which are located at different locations. Using optimal control methods, they derive optimal policies in terms of social contact restrictions and partial lockdown that will maximize economic output net of epidemic costs.

Adda et al. (2024) develop a joint model of disease diffusion and mental health. By linking mental health to preferences for mobility, they provide better micro-foundations of epidemic dynamics and use the model to provide empirical estimates using high-frequency and geolocalized data[36] on mobility and psychotropic drugs.

Brock and Xepapadeas (2025) develop an integrated model with two geographical regions, North and South, which captures interactions between the economy and the natural world and links climate, land use, and infectious diseases represented by SIS or SIR models. The SIS version of the integrated two-region $i = 1, 2$ model with population normalized to one is written as

$$\dot{S}_i(t) = -\beta_i(t) I_i(t) S_i(t) + \gamma_i I(t), \; S_i(0) > 0 \tag{25}$$

$$\dot{I}_i(t) = \beta_i(t) I_i(t) S_i(t) - \gamma_i I_i(t), \; I_i(0) > 0 \tag{26}$$

$$I_i(t) + S_i(t) = 1, \; i = 1, 2. \tag{27}$$

In this model, the quantity $\sigma_i(t) = \lambda_i(t)/\gamma_i$ is the regional basic reproduction number, which is defined as the average number of secondary infections produced when one infected individual is introduced into a host population where everyone is susceptible. Spatial interactions are realized through the contact number. The susceptible steady state is defined as

$$S_i(t) = \min\{1, 1/\sigma_i(t)\} \tag{28}$$

---

[35] See also Milner and Zhao (2008) for an SIR model with spatial diffusion.

[36] For the use of data in mathematical epidemiology models, see, for example, Arino (2020).

$$\frac{1}{\sigma_i(t)} = \phi_{0i}(R_1(t), T_1(t)) + \phi_{1i}\left[b_i v_i(t) - m_i^{as} S_i(t) - q_j(1 - S_{jt})\right] \quad (29)$$

$$i, j = 1, 2, \ i \neq j.$$

In (29), $\phi_{0i}(R_1(t), T_1(t))$ is the part of the inverse of the contact number that depends on variables evolving in the long run, namely land use and temperature in region 1, which is the infectious disease hot spot. The second term on the right-hand side of (29) indicates short-run effects from disease containment policies, where ϕ_{1i} characterizes the overall containment effectiveness, $v_i(t)$ is containment control such as vaccination or social distancing, b_i is the effectiveness of such control policies, and m_i^{as} denotes the rate of potential spread of the disease by asymptomatic infecteds. Individuals from one region can make short visits to the other by regular means of transportation (e.g., airplanes, ships). Infected individuals from region j traveling to region i infect individuals in region i proportionally to those infected in region j and vice versa, with proportionalities (q_j, q_i) respectively. The model is closed with an objective function which is defined in terms of a consumption composite and the natural environment. This objective is maximized subject to disease dynamics, climate dynamics, and land-use choices. The results suggest that the emergence of infectious diseases associated with land-use change and climate change points towards policies that will preserve the natural world (e.g., payments for ecosystem services); upwards adjustment of the social cost of carbon to capture the climate change–infectious disease link; and support of land augmenting innovations in agriculture that will slow down conversion and promote ecosystem conservation. Furthermore, the potential value of the ecosystem in mitigating future infectious diseases should be included in valuation studies based on stated preferences methods.

6 Spatially Differentiated Regulation for Transboundary and Global Externalities

This section focuses more on the regulation of transboundary local and global externalities. The modeling of local transboundary externalities is used as a natural introduction to the explicit spatial modeling of climate change.

6.1 Regulating a Transboundary Externality

We consider a simple transboundary[37] (or cross-border) – but not global – externality with local damages in a two-region model, which is a special case

---

[37] See La Torre et al. (2021) for a transboundary pollution problem with pollution diffusion.

of the general dispersion models described above with $d_{12} = D > 0$ and $d_{21} = 0$. A very simple model of transboundary pollution is used in order to stress the fact that optimal policies should have a spatial structure even when regions are symmetric in their fundamentals. Our approach, despite its simplicity, makes clear the impact of spatial transport on optimal environmental policies, and the core model presented below can be extended along many different lines.

Let $u_i(c_i) = \ln\left(y_i E_i^{\alpha} e^{-v_i(P_i)}\right), i = 1,2$, denote utility in region i from using emissions or energy E_i in production net of pollution damages, where y_i is an exogenous process incorporating the impact of other factors of production. Capital accumulation is not considered in order to simplify dynamics. The use of E accumulates a pollutant P_i in each region. Some of the pollutant accumulated in region 1 is transported to region 2 through natural forces (e.g., river flows, winds). The accumulated pollutant in each region generates damages according to a convex damage function $v_i(P_i), v_i' > 0, v_i'' \geq 0$. Pollution dynamics, with the explicit dependence on t omitted to ease notation, can be written as

$$\dot{P}_1 = -BP_1 - DP_1 + E_1 , \ P_1(0) = P_{10} \text{ given} \tag{30}$$

$$\dot{P}_2 = -BP_2 + DP_1 + E_2 , \ P_2(0) = P_{20} \text{ given,} \tag{31}$$

where $D > 0$ is the pollution transportation coefficient, or diffusivity, and $B > 0$ is a pollution depreciation rate. A regulator or a social planner will determine emission paths and emission taxes by maximizing the sum of discounted regional utilities subject to pollution dynamics.

The Hamiltonian representation of the regulator's problem with a quadratic damage function, $v_i(P_i) = c_{1i}P_i + (c_{2i}/2) P_i^2, i = 1,2$, can then be written as

$$\max_{E_i} \mathcal{H} = \max_{E_i} \left\{ \sum_{i=1,2} w_i \left[\alpha \ln E_i - v_i(P_i)\right] \right. \tag{32}$$

$$\left. + \mu_1 \left(-BP_1 - DP_1 + E_1\right) + \mu_2 \left(-BP_2 + DP_1 + E_2\right) \right\},$$

where $w_i, \sum_i w_i = 1$ are regional welfare weights.

Assume that each region is populated by identical atomistic agents that we represent by a representative agent in each region. Each such agent maximizes their own utility ignoring climate impacts on their own region as well as the other region. Thus they only optimize over energy use. The socially optimal solution resulting from problem (32) can be implemented with regional emission taxes solving the consumer's problem with Hamiltonian representation

$$\max_{E_i} \mathcal{H}_i = \max_{E_i} \{\ln(c_i)\} = \max_{E_i} \left\{\ln\left(y_i E_i^{\alpha} - \tau_i E_i + Tr_i\right)\right\}, \tag{33}$$

where Tr_i denotes lump sum transfers to the representative agent in region i. By combining the optimality conditions of problems (32) and (33), the optimal regional emission tax and transfers are

$$\tau_i = y_i \alpha \left(\frac{-w_i \alpha}{\mu_i} \right)^{\alpha-1} , \quad Tr_i = y_i \alpha \left(\frac{-w_i \alpha}{\mu_i} \right)^{\alpha-1} \left(\frac{-w_i \alpha}{\mu_i} \right). \tag{34}$$

As usual, regional emission taxes, $\tau = (\tau_1, \tau_2)$, are determined by the costate variables of the current value Hamiltonian, (μ_1, μ_2), which are negative since these variables express the marginal cost of the accumulated pollution, that is, the cost of the externality. The optimality conditions are shown in Appendix F. For the general case in which regions are asymmetric, regional taxes will be different. However, unidirectional pollution transport induces regionally differentiated optimal emission taxes even under full symmetry with respect to pollution damages, pollution dynamics, welfare weights, and exogenous endowments y_i across regions. The following results can be obtained.

Proposition 1

1. *With constant marginal damages, $c_2 = 0$, optimal emissions and emission taxes at a steady state are the same in both regions.*
2. *With linear and increasing marginal damages, $c_2 > 0$, emission taxes are different between regions. If $D \geq B$, then, $|\mu_1| > |\mu_2|$ which implies $0 < \tau_1 < \tau_2$. When $D < B$, then $0 < \tau_1 \lessgtr \tau_2$.*

For proof, see Appendix F.

Result 1 follows from the fact that the amount of social cost "saved" in region 1 because pollution is transported to region 2 is equal to the amount of social cost increase in region 2 because of the transported pollution.

Result 2 implies that when the pollution flux from region 1 to region 2 is stronger than pollution depreciation, then a regulator that weights regional welfare equally and maximizes global welfare will tax emissions in region 2 relatively more than in region 1. Region 2 is a high pollution accumulation region due to the unidirectional transport, so by taxing region 2 more, the regulator seeks to reduce pollution accumulation in region 2 by restricting emissions generated in 2. This is a rather unexpected result, since relatively higher taxation in region 1 – which generates the transported pollution – might have been expected. However, since the marginal social cost of pollution is now increasing in the amount of pollution, the "Coase"-type argument suggests that the reduction in social cost in region 1 from transport of some of its pollution to region 2 exactly cancels out and the social cost increase in region

2 no longer applies. With increasing marginal cost from the added pollution from transport, it is possible that at a certain point marginal cost will increase in region 2 more than the reduction in marginal cost in region 1. In this case, it is optimal to tax emissions generated in region 2 relatively more.[38]

To express the optimal taxes in consumption terms, the taxes should be divided by the marginal utility of consumption in each region. If consumption levels are different, there will be a further differentiation of the optimal pollution taxes. Thus, even in this simple two-region symmetric model, spatial transport of pollution implies that optimal taxes could, under reasonable assumptions, be spatially dependent.

In a symmetric two-region model with constant marginal damages, the steady state for the regional pollution accumulation and the corresponding social pollution cost is a global saddle point.[39] This means that for any two initial states of regional pollution accumulation, the regulator can calculate initial values for the social pollution cost, and therefore initial values and time paths for the optimal regional pollution taxes, so that the regulated system will converge to the optimal steady-state regional pollution accumulation. For the proof, see Appendix F.

The same results can be obtained under the assumption that each region can borrow and lend, b_i, at rate r. In this case, the Hamiltonian representation of the representative consumer's problem in each region will be

$$\max_{E_i} \mathcal{H}_i = \max_{E_i} \left\{ \ln(c_i) + \mu_{b_i} \left(rb_i + y_i E_i^{\alpha} - \tau_i E_i + Tr_i - c_i \right) \right\}.$$

Combining the optimality conditions with the planner's problem will provide the same regional taxes and transfers as in (34).

6.1.1 A Hybrid Model of Transboundary Pollution with Spatial Diffusion and Spillovers

The discussion about transboundary pollution can be combined in a model with the concepts of diffusion and spatial spillovers discussed above. Consider that in the optimization problem represented in (32), space is continuous, finite and linear $x \in [0, L]$, and that: (i) positive productivity spillovers of the

---

[38] For an early analysis of uniform versus differentiated regulation in a static context, see, for example, Kolstad (1987).

[39] Under saddle point stability, the regulator can choose initial values $\mu_i(0) = \phi_i(P_{10}, P_{20})$, $i = 1, 2$, so that the trajectories $((P_1(t)), P_2(t), \mu_1(t), \mu_2(t)), t \geq 0$ converge on a two-dimensional stable manifold generated by the eigenspace of the two negative eigenvalues of the Hamiltonian system, to the socially optimal steady state. Since the $-\mu_i(0)$ determine the initial emission taxes, the regulator can calculate the optimal paths for emission taxes and emissions.

type introduced by Lucas (2001) from the use of emissions or energy exist, modeled as

$$e^{z(x)} \text{ with } z(x) = \delta \int_0^L e^{-\delta(x-x')} E(x')\, dx',$$

and (ii) pollution diffuses following a Fickian diffusion process modeled by $D\partial_{xx}P(x)$. The social planner maximizes benefits over the whole spatial domain and the Hamiltonian for this problem, omitting t to ease notation, is

$$\mathcal{H} = \int_0^L w(x) \left\{ \left[\ln \left(y(x) E(x)^\alpha\, e^{-v(x)P(x)} e^{z(x)} \right) \right] \right.$$
$$\left. + \mu(x) [E(x) - mP(x) + D\partial_{xx}P(x)] \right\} dx.$$

Applying the maximum principle from Section 3, we obtain

$$E^*(x) = \frac{\alpha w(x)}{-\mu(x) - \delta S^{E(x)}}, \quad S^{E(x)} = \int_0^L e^{-\delta(x-x')^2}\, dx' \tag{35}$$

$$\partial_t \mu(x) = (\rho + m)\,\mu(x) + v(x) - D\partial_{xx}\mu(x) \tag{36}$$

$$\partial_t P(x) = E^*(x) - mP(x) + D\partial_{xx}P(x). \tag{37}$$

When atomistic representative agents in each site do not take into account the pollution and the productivity externality, the optimal site-specific pollution tax is

$$\tau^*(x; \alpha) = y(x)\,\alpha \left(\frac{w(x)\,\alpha}{-\mu(x) - \delta S^{E(x)}} \right)^{\alpha-1}. \tag{38}$$

In this case, even with flat earth $y(x) = y$ and equal weights $w(x) = w$, the pollution tax is site specific because pollution diffusion and spatial spillovers induce spatial structure in $\mu(x)$ and $S^{E(x)}$. A steady-state spatial distribution for $P(x), \mu(x)$ obtained from system (35)–(37) for $\partial_t \mu(x) = 0, \partial_t P(x) = 0$ is shown in Figure 4.[40] At the center of the spatial domain, the stock of pollution is high and its shadow cost is also high, indicating higher emissions taxes. The size of the emission tax is reduced by the spillover effect as indicated by (38), which reveals the trade-off between the productivity benefits from clustering emissions and the environmental cost of clustering pollution.

The parameters that were used to produce Figure 4 are: $L = 2\pi, p = 0.01$, $a = 0.3, m = 0.05, D = 1, v = 0.1, \delta = 0.01$.

This hybrid model can be extended in many directions to become more realistic, but this example clearly indicates how different transport mechanisms that act on real spatial phenomena could be combined in modeling and thus provide insights for policy design.

---

[40] The simulation is provided for illustration purposes only. It does not refer to a real example.

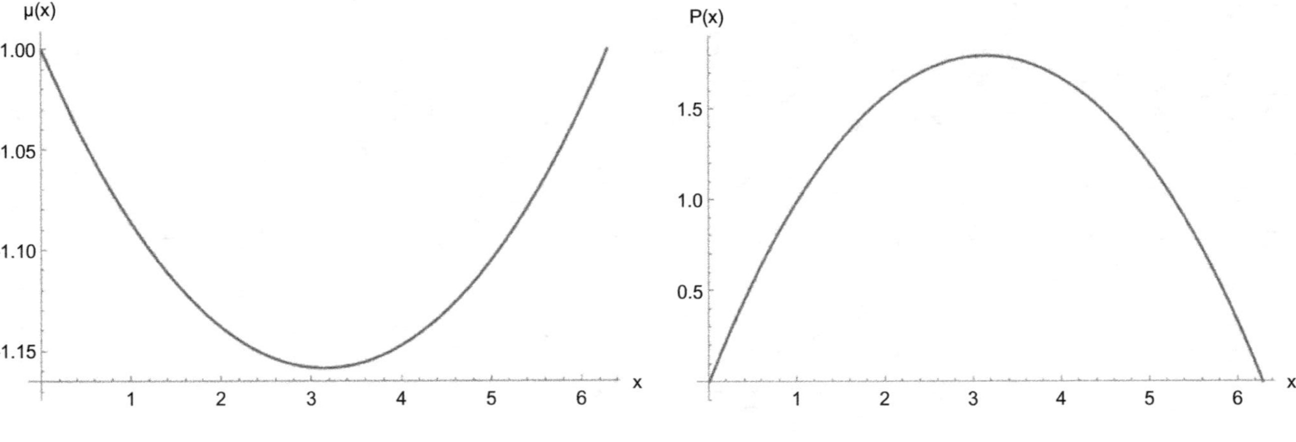

Figure 4   (a) The shadow cost of pollution $\mu(x)$. (b) The stock of pollution $P(x)$.

6.2 Regulating a Global Externality and Designing Global Climate Policy

The need for regional analysis of the impacts of climate change, in contrast to the global approach taken by integrated assessment models (IAMs) such as the Dynamic Integrated Model of Climate and the Economy (DICE) (Nordhaus and Sztorc, 2013; Nordhaus, 2014), has been clearly recognized in the literature (see, for example, Easterling, 1997). In fact, major IAMs such as the Regional Integrated Climate-Economy model (RICE) (e.g., Nordhaus, 2011), the Climate Framework for Uncertainty, Negotiation and Distribution (FUND) (e.g., Anthoff and Tol, 2013), or Policy Analysis of the Greenhouse Effect (PAGE) (e.g., Hope, 2006) explicitly include regional components. The regional aspects have been extended to both regional temperature effects and regional economic effects (e.g., FUND, PAGE), or to regional economic effects with predictions about mean global temperature (e.g., RICE). Multi-region modeling in climate change economics has been developed since RICE. Desmet and Rossi-Hansberg (2015) developed a spatial model of climate change, Krusell and Smith (2022) introduced a 20,000-region spatial model, and Hassler and Krusell (2018) discuss approaches to multi-region climate modeling.

6.2.1 Pattern Scaling

An approach that climate science uses to generate spatial temperature variation across regions is pattern or statistical downscaling, or statistical emulation methods (e.g., Castruccio et al., 2014; Hassler et al., 2016; Krusell and Smith, 2022). Pattern scaling assumes that all regional temperature anomalies relative to the preindustrial temperature in region i, T_{i0} defined as $T_i(t) - T_{i0}$, are proportional to the global mean temperature anomaly $T_{GM}(t) - T_{GM,0}$. That is,

$$T_i(t) - T_{i0} = \alpha_i \left[T_{GM}(t) - T_{GM,0} \right].$$

Castruccio et al. (2014) fit the equation

$$T_t = \beta_0 + \beta_1 \frac{1}{2} \left[\ln \frac{CO_{2,t}}{CO_{2,0}} + \ln \frac{CO_{2,t-1}}{CO_{2,0}} \right] + \beta_2 \sum_{k=2}^{k=t} \rho^k \ln \frac{CO_{2,t-k}}{CO_{2,0}} + \varepsilon_t$$

$$\varepsilon_t = \varphi \varepsilon_{t-1} + \sigma z_t , \quad \{z_t\} \text{ IIDN } (0,1),$$

where T_0 is given, $CO_{2,t}$ is concentration of CO_2 at t, and $CO_{2,0}$ is preindustrial concentration, to regional yearly temperature data generated by their atmosphere–ocean general circulation model (AOGCM) for one scenario to "train" their emulator. They then use their estimated equation for that scenario to mimic the output of their AOGCM for another scenario. They do this procedure for 47 regions (for estimates, see Castruccio et al. [2014, Table S1]). They estimate regressions of the form

$$T((L,l),t) - T_0(L,l) = \alpha_{(L,l)} \left[T_i(t) - T_{i,0} \right] + \varepsilon_{(L,l)},$$

where (L,l) denote longitude and latitude respectively. Performance measures suggest that the emulator does a fairly good job of mimicking the output of the much more complicated AOGCM. Figure 6 in Castruccio et al. (2014) displays the emulated temperatures with the top of the display corresponding to the northern latitude regions and the bottom to the southern latitude regions. The pattern of higher temperatures as one moves toward the northern regions is clear.

6.2.2 Heat and Precipitation Transport: Two- and Three-Box Models

Regional aspects of climate change and associated policies have been introduced in low-dimensional IAMs in which regional temperature dynamics are driven by endogenous mechanisms of heat and precipitation transport from the equator to the poles (Brock et al., 2013; Brock and Xepapadeas, 2017, 2019; Cai et al., 2019). The climate science part of these models is based on one- or two-dimensional dynamic energy balance climate models (EBCMs), defined either in discrete space in the context of South-North "two-box" models (e.g., Langen and Alexeev, 2007), or in continuous space (e.g., North et al., 1981). EBCMs generate spatial variability of temperature across regions through the endogenous mechanism of heat transfer.

Regional temperature differentiation also emerges from the use of the transient climate response to cumulative carbon emissions (TCRE) on a regional basis. The TCRE embodies both the physical effect of CO_2 on climate and the biochemical effect of CO_2 on the global carbon cycle (e.g., Matthews et al., 2009; Matthews et al., 2012; Knutti, 2013; Knutti and Rogelj, 2015; MacDougall and Friedlingstein, 2015; MacDougall et al., 2017). The TCRE, denoted by Λ, is defined as $\Lambda = \Delta T(t)/CE(t)$, where $CE(t)$ denotes cumulative carbon emissions up to time t and $\Delta T(t)$ denotes the change in temperature during the same period with $\Lambda = 1.7 \pm 0.4°C$ per TtC (Leduc et al., 2016). The approximate constancy of the TCRE suggests an approximately linear relationship between a change in global average temperature and cumulative emissions. This roughly linear relationship has also been recognized by the IPCC (2013).

Leduc et al. (2016) identify an approximately linear relationship between cumulative CO_2 emissions and regional temperatures. This relationship is quantified by regional TCREs, or RTCREs. The RTCRE parameters range from less than 1°C per TtC for some ocean regions to 5°C per TtC in the Arctic. The authors consider their approach to be a novel application of pattern scaling.

Heat and moisture transport from the equator to the poles, when combined with the surface-albedo feedback, results in the observed phenomenon of polar or Arctic amplification (IPCC, 2013: 396).[41] Arctic amplification could cause serious detrimental environmental effects which could be diffused to other regions south of the Arctic. Thus one implication of adopting a regional representation of climate is that changes in the temperature in one region could generate damages in another region. The existence of geographical spillover damage effects across regions is supported by recent studies.[42] If the stronger anomaly growth in the Arctic relative to the equator could cause damages in the South due to sea level rise or extreme weather phenomena, then local damages should depend on the local temperature anomalies in both regions. At the same time, heat transfer from the South to the North might benefit the South by reducing temperature levels in the relatively more vulnerable areas around the equator. For example, if heat transfer from the equator to the poles did not exist, then damages from extreme heat documented by Hsiang et al. (2017) in the low latitudes might be even larger and mortalities from both extreme heat in the low latitudes and extreme cold in the high latitudes documented by Gasparrini et al. (2015) might be even larger.

Detailed work on estimating marginal temperature and damage impacts due to spatial temperature differentials is an area for further research, since it will be needed in order to compute the impacts on optimal policy. Thus the issue of explicit consideration of heat transfer mechanisms in coupled models of climate and the economy could be important for policy purposes but, to our knowledge, has not been explicitly addressed by large-scale IAMs.

The two-box framework with meridional heat and moisture transport[43] with box $i = 1$, which is the South $(0°, 30°N)$, and box $i = 2$, which is the North $(30°N, 90°N)$, combined with the RTCRE approach, implies the following regional dynamics for the temperature anomalies:

$$\dot{T}_1 = \frac{1}{H}\left[(-B_1 - \gamma_1 - \gamma_2)T_1 + \gamma_1 T_2 + \Lambda_1 E\right],\ T_1(0) = 0 \tag{39}$$

---

[41] Bekryaev et al. (2010), using an extensive data set of monthly surface air temperature, document a high-latitude ($> 60°N$) warming rate of 1.36°C/century for 1875–2008, with the trend being almost two times stronger than the Northern Hemisphere trend of 0.79°C/century. The high RTCRE in the Arctic reported by Leduc et al. (2016) is indicative of Arctic amplification.

[42] See, for example, Francis and Vavrus (2014), Francis and Skific (2015), Francis (2017), Francis et al. (2018), and Wu and Francis (2019). The main message is that further Arctic warming may favor persistent weather patterns that can lead to weather extremes.

[43] For details, see Alexeev et al. (2005), Langen and Alexeev (2007), and Alexeev and Jackson (2013).

$$\dot{T}_2 = \frac{1}{H}\left[(\gamma_1 + \gamma_2)T_1 - (B + \gamma_1)T_2 + \Lambda_2 E\right], \quad T_2(0) = 0 \tag{40}$$

$$E = E_1 + E_2, \tag{41}$$

where (E_1, E_2) are regional carbon emissions, H is heat capacity, and (Λ_1, Λ_2) are the local TCRE in the South and North respectively.[44] Note that with $\gamma_1 = \gamma_2 = 0$, the temperature dynamics model (39)–(41) is reduced to the Leduc et al. (2016) model, while for $\Lambda_1 = \Lambda_2 = \Lambda$ it is reduced to the Langen and Alexeev (2007) model.

If a social planner seeks to maximize global welfare by choosing the paths of regional carbon emissions $E_i(t)$, the planner's objective, considering a log-utility function similar to the transboundary problem, is:

$$\max_{E_1, E_2} \int_0^\infty e^{-\rho t}\left[\sum_{i=1,2} w_i\left[\ln y_i + \alpha \ln E_i - \upsilon_i(T_1, T_2)\right]\right] dt \tag{42}$$

subject to (39)–(41),

where w_i represent as before welfare weights. Damages in each region depend on the temperature anomaly in the other region. This modeling seeks to capture effects such as damages in the South for the faster temperature increase in the Arctic, which may increase the frequency or/and the severity of extreme weather phenomena.

In a world with frictionless transfer of resources across regions and unlimited fossil fuels, the solution of the global externality problem (42) can be implemented, following the approach in the previous section, by carbon taxes and transfers defined as:

$$\tau_i = y_i \alpha \left(\frac{w_i \alpha H}{\mu_1 \Lambda_1 + \mu_2 \Lambda_2}\right)^{\alpha-1},$$

$$Tr_i = \left[y_i \alpha \left(\frac{w_i \alpha H}{\mu_1 \Lambda_1 + \mu_2 \Lambda_2}\right)^{\alpha-1}\right]\left(\frac{w_i \alpha H}{\mu_1 \Lambda_1 + \mu_2 \Lambda_2}\right).$$

The following result is straightforward. When welfare weights are equal, regional emissions are equal, therefore $\tau_1 < \tau_2$ if $y_1 < y_2$, and in this case the poorer region should pay a lower carbon tax. The size of carbon taxes depends on the shadow cost of regional temperature anomalies (μ_1, μ_2). In Appendix F, the Hamiltonian system for problem (42) with quadratic damage functions is presented. The impact of heat and precipitation transport can be analyzed by comparative analysis of parameters (γ_1, γ_2). Since in the poorer region $C_1 < C_2$, the poorer region will pay a lower carbon tax in consumption terms since

---

[44] The parameter values for the climate model can be obtained from calibrations of climate science models (e.g., Langen and Alexeev, 2007; Leduc et al., 2016).

$$\tau_1^C = \frac{\tau_1}{u'(C_1)} < \tau_2^C = \frac{\tau_2}{u'(C_2)}.$$

In climate change policy, a uniform carbon tax or carbon price across locations is a common result, stemming from the global nature of the climate externality. This attitude seems to change, however, as more aspects of the climate and the economy are taken into account. The High-Level Commission on Carbon Prices (2017) report and Stiglitz (2019) recommend nonuniform carbon taxes, with carbon taxes being relatively higher in regions where consumers are disproportionately rich. Brock et al. (2014), in a continuous space model with heat transport polarward, show that optimal carbon taxes are higher in relatively richer regions in which the marginal utility of consumption is lower.

Cai et al. (2019) developed a novel stochastic North-South large-scale IAM, based on the DICE/RICE framework for the climate module, with meridional heat and moisture transport, sea level rise, permafrost thaw, and stochastic tipping points. Cai et al. (2019) introduce adjustment costs in the economic interactions across regions and show that if these adjustment costs are zero, then the regional carbon tax is the same across regions since the marginal return of capital is equated across regions. However, with nonzero adjustment costs between regions, the regional carbon tax is different across regions.

More recently Cai et al. (2023), using the framework of DICE-2016R (Nordhaus, 2017), developed a three-box model that includes the three regions of the North, the tropics, and the South. Regional temperature anomalies along with the global ocean anomaly relative to 1900 levels evolve in discrete time according to

$$T_{t+1,1}^{AT} = (1 - \xi_5)T_{t,1}^{AT} - \xi_2(T_{t,1}^{AT} - T_t^{OC}) + \xi_4(T_{t,2}^{AT} - T_{t,1}^{AT}) + (\xi_1 + \xi_6)F_t$$

$$T_{t+1,2}^{AT} = (1 - \xi_5)T_{t,2}^{AT} - \xi_2(T_{t,2}^{AT} - T_t^{OC}) - \frac{\xi_4}{2}(T_{t,2}^{AT} - T_{t,1}^{AT}) -$$

$$\frac{\xi_4}{2}(T_{t,2}^{AT} - T_{t,3}^{AT}) + (\xi_1 + \xi_7)F_t$$

$$T_{t+1,3}^{AT} = (1 - \xi_5)T_{t,3}^{AT} - \xi_2(T_{t,3}^{AT} - T_t^{OC}) - \frac{\xi_4}{2}(T_{t,2}^{AT} - T_{t,3}^{AT}) + \xi_1 F_t$$

$$T_{t+1}^{OC} = T_t^{OC} + \xi_3(T_{t,1}^{AT} - T_t^{OC}) + 2\xi_3(T_{t,2}^{AT} - T_t^{OC}) + \xi_3(T_{t,3}^{AT} - T_t^{OC}).$$

In the dynamic system, $T_{t,i}^{AT}, i = 1, 2, 3$ is the temperature anomaly in each of the three regions, T_t^{OC} is the global ocean anomaly, and the ξ parameters characterize flows among the regions and the ocean. Parameter ξ_4 captures additional spatial heat and moisture transport between the North/South and the tropics due to differences in the temperature anomalies. The global radiative force, F_t, is defined as $F_t = \eta \log_2 \left(\frac{M^{AT}}{M_*^{AT}} \right) + F_t^{EX}$, where M^{AT} stands for carbon concentration, M_*^{AT} is the preindustrial concentration, $\eta = 3.68$, and F^{EX} is the exogenous global non-CO_2 radiative forcing.

Regional and global welfare are defined respectively as

$$U_i = \sum_{t=0}^{\infty} \beta^t u\left(c_{t,i}\right) L_{t,i}, \; W = \sum_i U_i,$$

where $u\left(c_{t,i}\right)$ is utility of per capita consumption, $L_{t,i}$ is population, and β is the utility discount factor. Cooperate solutions corresponding to maximization of global welfare subject to economic and climatic constraints, which include the regional temperature dynamics, are determined along with noncooperative solutions corresponding to the OLNE solution concept. The three-box model provides new insights regarding the regional social cost of carbon and GDP evolution under cooperation or noncooperation when climate change impacts economic growth.

Another issue emerging in regional models of climate change with heat and moisture transport is whether ignoring such a phenomenon introduces bias in optimal climate policies. Brock and Xepapadeas (2017, 2019) and Cai et al. (2019) show that ignoring heat and moisture transport could introduce serious bias in the optimal carbon taxes. The direction of the bias depends crucially on whether the costs to the South – from the faster increase in temperature in the North caused by the surface albedo feedback and heat flux – exceed the benefits in the South from the reduction in the regional temperature due to heat transfer.

6.2.3 Strategic Behavior

In major IAMs that involve optimization at the global or regional level, such as DICE or RICE, the objective is the maximization of a global welfare criterion (as with DICE) or the sum of welfare criteria across regions (as with RICE). In the case of RICE, the solution for the given objective corresponds to a cooperative solution in which a social planner chooses emissions paths to maximize aggregate regional welfare subject to economic and climate constraints. This assumption implies that regions or countries have agreed, through some kind of an international agreement, to follow cooperative emission paths.[45]

This approach is useful in identifying optimal cooperative emission paths and indicating policy instruments such as carbon taxes to attain these paths. However, when it comes to the real world, countries or regions might not

---

[45] Relevant examples are the outcomes of the Conferences of the Parties, such as the Kyoto Protocol or the Paris Agreement, which provide an idea of such a cooperative solution in the real world.

be willing to follow a cooperative solution. Although they may recognize the impact of climate change on global welfare, a specific region or country might be willing to choose emission paths that will maximize own welfare, which will in general be gross benefits from using fossil fuels net of own climate damages. In this case, the appropriate solution concept is the solution of a noncooperative dynamic game. The explicit introduction of regional temperature dynamics makes the noncooperative solution concept more realistic since each country or region will try to design optimal policies by considering own temperature dynamics and not global temperature dynamics.

A noncooperative solution in the context of climate change is an equilibrium outcome in which countries maximize own welfare subject to economic and climatic constraints and assumptions about the climate policies of other countries. In terms of the objective (42), this means

$$\max_{E_i} \int_0^\infty e^{-\rho t} \left[\ln y_i + \alpha \ln E_i - v_i \left(T_1, T_2 \right) \right] dt \, , \, i = 1, 2, \tag{43}$$

subject to economic and climatic constraints, and assumptions about the paths of $E_j(t); i \neq j$.

Nordhaus and Yang (1996), in the context of the RICE model, were the first to study noncooperative outcomes using the solution concept of the OLNE in which each country sets its climate policy to maximize its own economic welfare, assuming that other countries' policies are invariant to its policies. Dutta and Radner (2006), in a game-theoretic approach to global warming, consider models with multiplicity of equilibria which allow the identification of "Pareto-improving" equilibria. Bosetti et al. (2006) also derive OLNE solutions in the context of the regional World Induced Technical Change Hybrid model (better known as the WITCH model).[46]

Noncooperative solutions in general indicate that emissions will be higher and carbon taxes lower relative to the cooperative solutions. The earlier literature, although dealing with regional models, did not explicitly include heat transfer. Brock and Xepapadeas (2019) consider strategic interactions in a simple two-box model with heat transfer and damages in one region affected by the temperature in the other region, to capture impacts of Arctic amplification in the South. In addition to the OLNE, they also examine the FBNE.[47]

---

[46] For a detailed exposition of cooperative and noncooperative solutions in the context of integrated assessment modeling, see Yang (2008).

[47] It is well known that the OLNE does not possess the Markov perfect property and is not robust against unexpected changes in the state of the system. Thus a feedback equilibrium is considered to be a more satisfactory solution. With an open loop information structure, each region takes the emission path of the other region as given. In a feedback structure, each

Cai et al. (2019) use a novel algorithm to determine the FBNE in the stochastic two-region model described above, which contains 11 state variables and eight decision variables, while Cai et al. (2023) explicitly solve the OLNE of a three-box model.

The main message from the two-region climate models with heat and moisture transfer is that in both cooperative and noncooperative solutions, ignoring the transport mechanism – which is a well-established mechanism – could introduce serious biases in climate policy.

6.2.4 Heat and Precipitation Transport: One-Dimensional Continuous-Space Models

Two-region climate models provide important insights into the role of transport mechanisms in the design of climate policy. Similar insights can also be provided by more detailed EBCMs in continuous space. EBCMs are distinguished into wet models in which temperature diffusion is replaced by moist static energy diffusion (e.g., Flannery, 1984), and dry models in which the basic thermodynamic variable used to determine energy transport is temperature (e.g., Sellers, 1969; North, 1975a, 1975b; Ghil, 1976; North et al., 1981; Ghil and Lucarini, 2020). In both models, energy transports generate polar amplification under different assumptions.

Following Merlis and Henry (2018), and dropping t to ease notation, a wet EBCM is written as

$$C\partial_t T(\phi) = \frac{1}{4}QS(\phi)a(\phi) - [A + BT(\phi)] - \nabla \cdot \mathbf{F}_a(\phi) + \mathcal{F}, \tag{44}$$

where C is heat capacity; T is surface temperature; ϕ is latitude;[48] Q is the solar constant; $S(\phi)$ is the insolation structure function; $a(\phi)$ is the coalbedo; $[A+BT(\phi)]$ is outgoing long-wave radiation; $\mathcal{F}$ is radiative forcing; and $\nabla \cdot \mathbf{F}_a = -\partial_x \left[\mathcal{D}\left(1 - x^2\right)\partial_x h(x)\right]$ with $x = \sin\phi$ is the divergence of the atmospheric energy flux, which is governed by the diffusion of the moist static energy h measured in units of temperature, with diffusivity $\mathcal{D}$.

In dry EBCMs, the term $\nabla \cdot \mathbf{F}_a$ is replaced by $-\partial_x \left[\mathcal{D}\left(1 - x^2\right)\partial_x T(x)\right]$ with ϕ replaced by x in the rest of the functions. The temperature spatiotemporal

---

region assumes that the emissions of the other region are a function of the current temperature anomalies or $E_i(t) = h_i(T_1(t), T_2(t), t)$.

The FBNE is derived in a dynamic programming framework (e.g., Başar and Olsder, 1995) and by construction is Markov perfect.

[48] When the spatial dimension is one, that is, latitude only, the EBCMs are called one-dimensional. In contrast, models without spatial transport mechanisms are called zero-dimensional.

dynamics described by (44) can be incorporated into an economic model of climate change by an appropriate specification of radiative forcing $\mathcal{F}$. Brock et al. (2013) and Brock et al. (2014, 2015) use (44) in a coupled model of the economy and the environment and define forcing using the standard relationship $\mathcal{F} = (\lambda/\ln 2)(\ln (S_t/S_0))$, where λ is climate sensitivity and S_t/S_0 is the ratio of the concentration of CO_2 in the atmosphere between period t and the preindustrial concentration S_0. They show that if welfare weights across locations are equal, then in cooperative solutions the location with the lower per capita consumption should pay lower carbon taxes, a result which is in line with Stiglitz (2019).

In the context of the approximate proportional relationship between changes in temperature and emissions, the optimization of a welfare objective subject to (44) can be simplified by using instead of $\mathcal{F}$ the term $\Lambda \int_{x=-1}^{x=1} E(x,t)\,dx$, where Λ is the TCRE and the integral term corresponds to global emissions at time t.[49]

Using an objective similar to (42), the planner's problem when a continuous-space one-dimensional dry EBCM with local TCRE is used to model climate can be written as

$$\max_{E_1 E_2} \int_0^\infty e^{-\rho t} \left[\int_{-1}^1 w(x)\left[\ln y(x) + \alpha \ln E(x) - \upsilon \left[T(x)\right]^2\right] dx \right] dt, \qquad (45)$$

subject to

$$C\partial_t T(x) = \frac{1}{4}QS(x)a(x) - [A + BT(x)] \qquad (46)$$

$$+ \partial_x \left[\mathcal{D}\left(1 - x^2\right)\partial_x T(x)\right] + \Lambda \int_{-1}^1 E(x)\,dx.$$

Optimal local emissions are determined as

$$E(x,t) = \frac{-\alpha w(x)}{\Lambda \int_{-1}^1 \mu(x)\,dx}. \qquad (47)$$

Using the heuristic proof for the derivation of the maximum principle, the Hamiltonian system of (45) implies that the local shadow cost of changes in temperature, which determines optimal emissions, evolves according to

$$\partial_t \mu(x) = (\rho + B)\mu(x) + \upsilon(x) + \partial_x \left[\mathcal{D}\left(1 - x^2\right)\partial_x \mu(x)\right],$$

along with (46) in which $E(x)$ is replaced by (47).

---

[49] In the linear approximation of local temperature change,

$$T(t, x) - T(t, 0) = \int_0^t \left[\Lambda \int_{-1}^1 E(x,t)\,dx\right] dt;$$

therefore, $\partial_t T(t, x) = \Lambda \int_{-1}^1 E(x,t)\,dx$.

If we assume again that each location x is populated by an identical representative agent that maximizes own utility ignoring climate impacts on own location as well as on the other locations, the socially optimal solution resulting from problem (45) can be implemented with latitude-specific carbon taxes of the form

$$\tau(x) = \alpha y(x) \left(\frac{\alpha w(x) C}{\Lambda \int_{-1}^{1} \mu(x)\, dx} \right)^{\alpha - 1}.$$

The problem which involves a Hamiltonian system in nonlinear PDEs can in principle be solved numerically. An approximation approach for solving this problem in terms of ODEs is presented in Appendix G.

6.2.5 Climate Change and Economic Geography

The spatial dimension of climate change policy becomes relevant when the fact that global greenhouse gas emissions affect local temperature and induce local damages is taken into account. Desmet and Rossi-Hansberg (2015) develop such a model in which temperature dynamics at location x and time t evolve as

$$T(x,t) = T(x,0) + v_1 S(t)^{v_2} (1 - v_3 T(x,0)),$$

where $S(t)$ is the stock of carbon in the atmosphere. Considering a two-sector economy – agriculture and manufacturing – in a half sphere representing the Northern hemisphere, they characterize a competitive equilibrium and through a calibration exercise they analyze how climate change affects the spatial distribution of economic activity, trade, migration, growth, and welfare.

Since the heterogeneity of effects emerges across countries but also within countries, models with detailed resolution of the geographical space have been developed. In a recent paper, Cruz and Rossi-Hansberg (2024) develop a economic geography model with $1°\text{x}1°$ resolution and estimate local damages associated with the impact of climate change on local productivity and amenities. The climate part in this model consists of the following equations:

$$S_{t+1} = S_{pre-ind} + \sum_{l=1}^{\infty} (1 - \delta_l) \left(E_{t+1-l}^{f} + E_{t+1-l}^{x} \right)$$

$$F_{t+1} = \lambda \log_2 \left(\frac{S_{t+1}}{S_{pre-ind}} \right) + F_{t+1}^{x},$$

where E_t^{f}, E_t^{x} are endogenous fossil-fuel-related emissions and exogenous CO_2 emissions respectively, $1 - \delta_l$ is the share of CO_2 emissions remaining in the atmosphere l periods ahead, $S_{pre-ind}$ is the preindustrial stock of greenhouse gases, λ is the equilibrium climate sensitivity (defined as the equilibrium near-surface temperature response to a doubling of atmospheric CO_2), F is the radiative forcing from an increase in the stock of carbon in the atmosphere relative to the preindustrial period, and F^x is radiative forcing from non-greenhouse gases. Then global temperature dynamics are defined as

$$T_{t+1} = T_{pre-ind} + \sum_{l=0}^{\infty} \zeta_l F_{t+1-l},$$

and local temperature dynamics at location x, using a pattern scaling approach, as

$$T_t(x) - T_{t-1}(x) = g(x)(T_t - T_{t-1}),$$

where the coefficient $g(x)$ indicates the change in the temperature of cell x, in °C when global average temperature changes by 1°C. The quantification of the model suggests, among other results, spatially heterogeneous losses from climate change with the largest part of the losses being in Africa and Latin America. Spatially uniform carbon taxes have heterogenous impacts across locations, with the regions that were projected to lose the most from global warming gaining from a carbon tax.

7 Uncertainty and Space

An issue that acquires importance in a spatial context is uncertainty. In recent papers, Barnett et al. (2020, 2022), Brock and Hansen (2019), and Hansen and Sargent (2019) distinguish three forms of uncertainty.

- Risk: The probabilities (objective or subjective) of uncertain outcomes are known, and the decision-maker is confident about the model used. Uncertainty exists within the model.
- Ambiguity: There are a large number of potential models that could be used by the decision-maker. There is a question regarding the decision-maker's level of confidence in each model.
- Misspecification: The question here is how the decision-maker uses models that are not perfect and may have unknown flaws.

Sometimes the last two forms are referred to as "deep uncertainty." Uncertainty could have a profound spatial structure, insofar as different forms of uncertainty or combinations of forms with spatially heterogeneous characteristics could prevail across locations. For a regulator seeking to derive optimal policies for the whole spatial domain, the spatial structure of uncertainty presents an additional challenge, since the policy should take into account spatial heterogeneities induced by transport mechanisms and uncertainty.

The robust control approach to uncertainty introduced to economics by Hansen and Sargent (e.g., 2001, 2008) is very convenient for extensions to situations in which the regulator faces uncertainty with different regional characteristics or, to put it in terms of robust control methods, the regulator has different misspecification concerns about different locations. These concerns could refer to local damages, pollution or resource dynamics, or diffusivity.

Brock et al. (2014c) study a robust control problem with site-specific misspecification concerns. Their main finding is the identification of specific sites, which they call "hot spots," in which serious concerns about misspecification could lead to the inability to define efficient regulation for the whole spatial domain. The emergence of "regulatory hot spots" acquires a high level of importance in the analysis of climate change because of the existence of tipping points (Lenton et al., 2008), which are locations associated with the triggering of big damages and which are surrounded by large uncertainties.

A brief exposition of modeling a spatial robust control problem can be presented in the following way. Brock and Xepapadeas (2018) use robust control to construct a regional policy that works uniformly well over a set of alternative models surrounding a "baseline" model. Intuitively the robust control method leads to the regulator maximizing against a "worst-case" model in the set of alternative models. The worst-case model is chosen by an adversarial agent that is trying to minimize the regulator's objective. Following Anderson et al. (2012) and Anderson et al. (2014), the stochastic robust control model can, under appropriate scaling, be transformed into a simpler deterministic robust control model.

Consider a multi-regional version of problem (42) and assume the regulator has concerns about misspecification in regional temperature dynamics, damages, and diffusivity. This can be interpreted as follows: The regulator has a benchmark model describing dynamics, spatial transport, and damages, but is not confident about the model and wants to regulate by taking into account the possibility that alternative models that represent distortions of the benchmark model could be realized as the actual model. To discipline the sensitivity analysis underlying the distortion of the parameters, the alternative models are contained in a bounded set and the adversarial agent chooses models/distortions to minimize the regulator's objective.

The spatial deterministic robust control problem can be defined as

$$
\max_{\{E_{it}\}} \min_{\{k_{it}, h_{it}\}} \tag{48}
$$

$$
\int_{t=0}^{\infty} e^{-\rho t} \sum_{i=1}^{N} w_i \left[\ln y_i + \alpha \ln E_{it} - \psi_i\left(T_{1t}, \ldots, T_{nt}, k_i\right) + \frac{k_{it}^2}{2\eta_i} + \frac{h_{it}^2}{2\theta_i} \right] dt,
$$

subject to

$$\dot{T}_{it} = \Lambda_i \sum_{i=1}^{N} E_{it} - B_i T_{it} + \sigma_i h_{it}, \ T_{i0} \geq 0. \tag{49}$$

In (48), $\psi_i\left(T_{1t},\ldots,T_{nt},k_i\right)$ is the damage function, the parameter σ_i represents volatility of regional temperature dynamics, h_{it} the corresponding drift distortion reflecting deep uncertainty, and θ_i the concerns about misspecification of temperature dynamics. The initial conditions reflect that T_{it} represents the temperature anomaly relative to a given base period. We assume that concerns about regional temperature dynamics are specific to the region, and therefore embody concerns about the RTCRE, which could also be an uncertain parameter. The k_i represents ambiguity about damages in region i, and η_i the concerns about misspecification of the damage function. Note that misspecification concerns are site specific and thus embody the different degree of uncertainty that the regulator faces across locations. Note also that the damage function in region i embodies geographical damage spillovers, or cross effects, which are damages caused by temperature increases in other regions. For example, the larger anomaly in the high northern latitudes may generate damages in terms of sea level rise or greenhouse gases emitted by permafrost melting in southern regions.

Optimal emissions are given by

$$E_{it}^* = \frac{-\alpha w_i}{\sum_i \Lambda_i \mu_{it}}.$$

The regional temperature shadow costs and the optimal emissions in this case are determined – through the Hamiltonian system – by the local misspecification concerns (η_i, θ_i). The same holds for the optimal site-specific taxes.

Brock and Xepapadeas (2020) develop and calibrate a three-region model with quadratic damages in temperature, spatial spillovers, and linear ambiguity impact on damage function, with the damage function defined as

$$\psi_i = \sum_{j=1}^{n}\left(d_{ij}T + \frac{1}{2}v_{ij}T_j^2 + k_{it}T_j\right),$$

where the coefficients $\left(d_{ij}, v_{ij}\right)$ represent spatial damage spillovers, and distributional weights are defined as

$$\omega_i = \left(\frac{\bar{y}}{y_i}\right)^e,$$

where $\bar{y}$ is world GDP per capita, y_i is GDP per capita in region i, and e is the elasticity of marginal utility. Results indicate that in general, robust policies under deep uncertainty lead to more conservative emission policies relative to a deterministic situation, or a situation of pure risk. Furthermore, ambiguity related to the damage function resulted in more conservative policies relative to ambiguity in temperature dynamics. The most vulnerable region benefits in welfare terms from robust policies when misspecification concerns are mild. Furthermore, the most vulnerable/poorest region pays a lower carbon tax when distribution across regions is taken into account. It is also shown that competitive firms, when facing ambiguity regarding carbon taxes, tend to be more conservative and use smaller amounts of fossil fuels relative to the case of no policy uncertainty. Policy uncertainty could be important in practice because it relates to uncertainties in the transition to a low-carbon economy. These results suggest that in the context of the Paris Agreement and the "Paris rulebook," it will be important to explore the issue of differentiated policy instruments, either carbon taxes or tradable permits, among rich and poor countries and the potential issues associated with the emergence of carbon leakage.

Spatial robust control methods can be extended to stochastic control problems, continuous spatial domain, and noncooperative solutions. Given the spatial differentiation of uncertainty across locations, this is a very interesting area for further research.

8 Concluding Remarks

Although the spatial dimension is embedded in the vast majority of issues studied by environmental and resource economics, its incorporation into economic models – especially in the form of explicit introduction of a spatial transport mechanism – is not widespread. There are a number of notable exceptions, many of which are discussed in this Element. Failure to explicitly incorporate the spatial dimension means that important aspects of the problem may not be accounted for, which could result in regulatory inefficiencies.

Furthermore, when it comes to policy design, accounting for the spatial dimension implies spatially dependent instruments and possibly the need for menus of instruments to deal with the potential emergence of various spatial externalities. Again, the lack of such instruments may result in inefficient policies.

The purpose of this Element, therefore, was threefold: to present the evolution of spatial methods in environmental and resource economics; to emphasize that space matters in the design of efficient policies; and to indicate future research areas where spatial methods could provide new and useful insights.

In this context, we presented the major spatial transport mechanisms and the way in which they can be incorporated into forward-looking optimizing economic models. We provided an extension of Pontryagin's maximum principle under spatial dynamics and explained how optimal Turing instability may emerge in this setup. Optimal Turing instability is a precursor to spatial pattern formation in the quantity-shadow price domain and provides the basis for introducing spatially dependent policies.

Moreover, we presented examples of the use of the framework of spatial dynamics that illustrate why space matters in environmental and resource economics, and how policy is differentiated when spatial transport mechanisms are taken into account. These examples include topics related to fishery management, groundwater management, pollution control, urban economics, climate policy, and the management of spatially structured uncertainty.

The tools presented in the Element, along with some examples of their application, provide a path for future research in spatial environmental and resource economics in which the underlying spatial dimension – which is very real – is fully taken into account.

Appendices

Appendix A

The PDE whose solution is shown in Figure 1a is

$$\frac{\partial y\,(t,x)}{\partial t} = r y(t,x)\left(1 - \frac{y(t,x)}{K}\right) - u y(t,x) + D\frac{\partial^2 y\,(t,x)}{\partial x^2}$$

$$t \in [0, 5000],\ \ x \in [0,\pi],\ \ y\,(0,x) = \sin(x)$$

$$y\,(t,0) = y\,(t,\pi) = 0,\ \text{hostile boundary}$$

$$r = 0.3, K = 10, u = 0.1, D = 0.03.$$

The reaction-diffusion system whose solution is shown in Figure 1c is

$$\frac{\partial y_1\,(t,x)}{\partial t} = r_1 y_1(t,x)\left(1 - \frac{y_1(t,x)}{K_1}\right) - \frac{\beta_1 y_2(t,x)}{y_1(t,x) + K_2}$$

$$- u_1 y_1(t,x) + D_1\frac{\partial^2 y_1\,(t,x)}{\partial x^2}$$

$$\frac{\partial y_2\,(t,x)}{\partial t} = r_2 y_2(t,x)\left(1 - \frac{\beta_2 y_2(t,x)}{y_1(t,x)}\right)$$

$$- u_2 y_2(t,x) + D_2\frac{\partial^2 y_2\,(t,x)}{\partial x^2}$$

$$t \in [0, 5000], x \in [0,\pi],\ y_1\,(0,x) = 1 + 2\sin(x),\ y_2\,(0,x) = 1.2 + \sin(x)$$

$$y_1\,(t,0) = y_1\,(t,\pi) = 1,\ y_2\,(t,0) = y_2\,(t,\pi) = 1.5$$

$$r_1 = 0.3, r_2 = 0.35, K_1 = 10, K_2 = 1, \beta_1 = \beta_2 = 1, u_1 = u_2 = 1,$$

$$D_1 = 0.03, D_2 = 0.02.$$

The PDE with advection whose solution is shown in Figure 1d is

$$\frac{\partial y\,(t,x)}{\partial t} = r y(t,x)\left(1 - \frac{y(t,x)}{K}\right) - \gamma\frac{\partial y\,(t,x)}{\partial x} - u y(t,x) + D\frac{\partial^2 y\,(t,x)}{\partial x^2}$$

$$\gamma = -0.12.$$

The composite kernel shown in Figure 2a is

$$w\,(x - x') = \exp\left(\alpha\,(x - x')^2\right) - \gamma\exp\left(\beta\,(x - x')^2\right),\ x, x' \in [-6\pi, 6\pi]$$

$$\alpha = -0.05, \gamma = 0.5, \beta = -0.02.$$

The integrodifferential equation, with the composite kernel used to derive Figure 2a whose solution is shown in Figure 2b, is

$$\frac{\partial y\,(t,x)}{\partial t} = ry(t,x)\left(1 - \frac{y(t,x)}{K}\right) - uy(t,x) - \frac{\delta y(t,x)^2}{1 + y(t,x)^2}$$

$$+ \phi \int_{-6\pi}^{6\pi} w\,(x - x')\,y\,(x - x')\,dx'$$

$$t \in [0, 5000],\; x \in [-6\pi, 6\pi],\; y\,(0, x) = 5 + \sin(x)$$

$$y\,(t, -6\pi) = y\,(t, 6\pi),\; \text{periodic boundary conditions (circle)}$$

$$r = 0.475, K = 10, u = 2, \delta = 0.1, \phi = 1.1.$$

All numerical solutions and their plots were obtained using the solver *NDSolve* of Mathematica 11.

Appendix B

A sketch of a heuristic proof of the maximum principle under diffusion can be presented by using a variational argument along the lines of Kamien and Schwartz (1991: 124–127). Considering a finite time horizon $t \in [t_0, t_1]$, problem (5) subject to (1) with appropriate spatial boundary conditions can be written as

$$J = \int_{\mathcal{O}} \int_{t_0}^{t_1} e^{-\rho t} U\,(y\,(t,x), u\,(t,x))\,dtdx$$

$$= \int_{\mathcal{O}} \int_{t_0}^{t_1} e^{-\rho t} \left\{ U\,(y\,(t,x), u\,(t,x)) \right.$$

$$\left. + p\,(t,x)\left[f\,(x\,(t,x), u\,(t,x)) + D\frac{\partial^2 y}{\partial x^2} - \frac{\partial y}{\partial t}\right]\right\} dtdx. \tag{50}$$

Integrate by parts the last two terms of (50) to express the terms $e^{-\rho t} p\,(t,x)\frac{\partial y}{\partial t}$ and $e^{-\rho t} p\,(t,x) D\frac{\partial^2 y}{\partial x^2}$ in terms of $y\frac{\partial p}{\partial t}$ and $\frac{\partial y}{\partial x}\frac{\partial p}{\partial t}$, integrate by parts once more to express the last term in terms of $y\,(t,x)\frac{\partial^2 p}{\partial x^2}$, and use spatial boundary and limiting intertemporal transversality conditions to eliminate constants. Introduce a one-parameter family of comparison controls $u^*\,(t,x) + \epsilon\eta\,(t,x)$, where $u^*\,(t,x)$ is the optimal control, $\eta\,(t,x)$ is a fixed function, and ϵ is a small parameter. Let $y\,(t,x,\epsilon)$, $t \in [t_0, t_1]$, $x \in \mathcal{O}$ be the smooth state variable generated by the diffusion process with control $u^*\,(t,z) + \epsilon\eta\,(t,z)$. Write $J\,(\epsilon)$ in terms of $y\,(t,x,\epsilon)$ and $u^*\,(t,x) + \epsilon\eta\,(t,x)$, and note that since u^* is a maximizing control, the function $J\,(\epsilon)$ assumes the maximum when $\epsilon = 0$ or $\left.\frac{dJ(\epsilon)}{d\epsilon}\right|_{\epsilon=0} = 0$. Performing the maximization and using transversality and spatial boundary conditions, we obtain the maximum principle.

For a sketch of a heuristic proof of the maximum principle under spatial kernels, write (5) subject to (2) as

$$J = \int_{\mathcal{O}} \int_{t_0}^{t_1} e^{-\rho t} U\left(y\left(t,x\right), u\left(t,x\right)\right) dt dx = \int_{\mathcal{O}} \int_{t_0}^{t_1} e^{-\rho t} \left\{ U\left(y\left(t,x\right), u\left(t,x\right)\right) \right.$$

$$\left. + p\left(t,x\right) \left[f\left(x\left(t,x\right), u\left(t,x\right), \mathbf{K}y\left(t,x\right)\right) - \frac{\partial y}{\partial t} \right] \right\} dt dx. \tag{51}$$

Integrate by parts the term $e^{-\rho t} p \frac{\partial y}{\partial t}$ and use spatial boundary and limiting intertemporal transversality conditions to eliminate constants. Introduce comparison controls $u^*\left(t,x\right) + \epsilon \eta\left(t,x\right)$ as before, with $Y\left(t,x,\epsilon\right) = \mathbf{K}y\left(\epsilon\right)$, define $J\left(\epsilon\right)$, calculate $\left. \frac{dJ(\epsilon)}{d\epsilon} \right|_{\epsilon=0} = 0$, and then use the linearity of the kernel operator to obtain the necessary conditions. For another way of deriving the Pontryagin maximum principle, see Xepapadeas and Yannacopoulos (2023).

Appendix C

Solution of a Linear Quadratic Problem (LQP) under Spatial Diffusion

Consider the following LQP with $\mathcal{O} = [0, L]$:

$$\max_{u(t,x)} \int_0^L \int_0^\infty e^{-\rho t} \left[-\frac{A}{2} y\left(t,x\right)^2 - \frac{B}{2} u\left(t,x\right)^2 + N y\left(t,x\right) u\left(t,x\right) \right] dt dx \tag{52}$$

$$A, B, \rho > 0, \ AB - N^2 > 0$$

$$\text{s.t.} \quad \frac{\partial y\left(t,x\right)}{\partial t} = F y\left(t,x\right) - G u\left(t,x\right) + D \frac{\partial^2 y\left(t,x\right)}{\partial x^2} \quad F, G > 0 \tag{53}$$

$$y\left(0,x\right) = y_0\left(x\right) \text{ given, } x \text{ in a circle } x \in [0, L] \tag{54}$$

$$y \text{ in a circle } x \in [0, L], y\left(t,0\right) = x\left(y, L\right) \text{ for all } t. \tag{55}$$

For the control problem (52)–(55), consider a set of controls $\mathcal{U}$ which have Fourier series expansions with piecewise continuous coefficients in t for nodes $n = 0, 1, 2, \ldots$, or

$$\mathcal{U} = \left\{ u\left(t,x\right) : u\left(t,x\right) = \sum_n \left[u_{1n}\left(t\right) \cos\left(\frac{2\pi n x}{L}\right) + u_{2n}\left(t\right) \sin\left(\frac{2\pi n x}{L}\right) \right] \right\}. \tag{56}$$

In this case, the solution of (52), under appropriate regularity assumptions for any $u\left(t,z\right) \in U$ will have a Fourier series expansion with piecewise continuously differentiable coefficients in t, or

$$y\left(t,x\right) = \sum_n \left[y_{1n}\left(t\right) \cos\left(\frac{2\pi n x}{L}\right) + y_{2n}\left(t\right) \sin\left(\frac{2\pi n x}{L}\right) \right] \tag{57}$$

$$p\left(t,x\right) = \sum_n \left[p_{1n}\left(t\right) \cos\left(\frac{2\pi n x}{L}\right) + p_{2n}\left(t\right) \sin\left(\frac{2\pi n x}{L}\right) \right]. \tag{58}$$

Substituting the $y(t, x)$ and $u(t, x)$ in (53), we obtain a set of transition equations parametrized by $n = 0, 1, 2, \ldots$.

As shown in Brock and Xepapadeas (2008), using the fact that the set of functions $\left\{\cos\left(\frac{2\pi nz}{L}\right), \sin\left(\frac{2\pi nz}{L}\right)\right\}, n = 0, 1, 2, \ldots$ is a complete orthogonal set over $[0, L]$, the following countable set of spatially independent optimal control problems for each $n = 0, 1, 2, \ldots$ can be obtained:

$$\max_{u_0(t)} \int_0^\infty e^{-\rho t}\left[-\frac{A}{2}y_0^2 - \frac{B}{2}u_0^2 + Ny_0u_0\right]dt \tag{59}$$

subject to $\dot{y}_0 = Fy_0 - Gu_0 \, , \, n = 0 \tag{60}$

$$\max_{u_{1n}(t)} \frac{L}{2} \int_0^\infty e^{-\rho t} \sum_n \left[-\left(\frac{A}{2}y_{1n}^2 + \frac{B}{2}u_{1n}^2\right) + Ny_{1n}u_{1n}\right]dt \tag{61}$$

subject to $\dot{y}_{1n} = S(k)y_{1n} - Gu_{1n} \, , n = 1, 2, \ldots \tag{62}$

$$\max_{u_{2n}(t)} \frac{L}{2} \int_0^\infty e^{-\rho t} \sum_n \left[-\left(\frac{A}{2}y_{2n}^2 + \frac{B}{2}u_{2n}^2\right) + Ny_{2n}u_{2n}\right]dt \tag{63}$$

subject to $\dot{y}_{2n} = S(k)y_{2n} - Gu_{2n} \, , n = 1, 2, \ldots \tag{64}$

$$S(k) = F - D\left(\frac{2\pi n}{L}\right)^2 = F - Dk^2 \, , k = \frac{2\pi n}{L}. \tag{65}$$

The solutions $\{y_{in}^*, p_{in}\}, i = 1, 2$, and finite number of nodes n should be substituted back into (56), (57), and (58) to obtain the optimal spatiotemporal paths for $y(t, x)$, $p(t, x)$, and $u(t, x)$.

Nonlinear quadratic problems require numerical solutions. For a solution of the LQP using dynamic programming, see Boucekkine et al. (2019a).

Appendix D

Emergence of Optimal Diffusion Instability

The maximized current value Hamiltonian or pre-Hamiltonian for the flat LQ system $(D = 0)$, where we drop subscripts and superscripts to simplify notation, is

$$H^0(y, p) = \max_u \left\{-\frac{A}{2}y^2 - \frac{B}{2}u^2 + Nyu + p[Fy - Gu]\right\}. \tag{66}$$

The Jacobian of the Hamiltonian system at the FOSS (y^*, p^*) is defined as[50]

$$J^0\left(y^*,p^*\right) = \begin{bmatrix} H^0_{yp}\left(y^*,p^*\right) & H^0_{pp}\left(y^*,p^*\right) \\ -H^0_{yy}\left(y^*,p^*\right) & \rho - H^0_{py}\left(y^*,p^*\right) \end{bmatrix}$$

$$= \begin{bmatrix} F - \frac{GN}{B} & \frac{G^2}{B} \\ A - \frac{N^2}{B} & \rho - F + \frac{GN}{B} \end{bmatrix}. \tag{67}$$

Theorem 1 gives one set of sufficient conditions for diffusion-induced instability of optimal control.

Theorem 1 (Optimal Turing Instability) *Assume that in the LQP with $D = 0$, the FOSS (y^*,p^*) associated with the Jacobian matrix $J^0\left(y^*,p^*\right)$ has the local saddle point property. Then, if*

$$\alpha \equiv \left(F - \frac{GN}{B}\right) > \frac{\rho}{2} \tag{68}$$

$$\frac{\rho^2}{4} > \left(A - \frac{N^2}{B}\right)\left(\frac{G^2}{B}\right) \equiv \beta, \tag{69}$$

there is a $D > 0$ such that the negative eigenvalue of the linearization

$$\mathbf{w}_t = J^0\mathbf{w} + \tilde{D}\mathbf{w}_{xx}, \tilde{D} = \begin{pmatrix} D & 0 \\ 0 & -D \end{pmatrix}, \tag{70}$$

where $\mathbf{w} = (y(t,x) - y^*, p(t,x) - p^*)$, becomes positive. That is, both eigenvalues of the Jacobian matrix in (70) have positive real parts. Thus diffusion locally destabilizes the FOSS, and optimal dynamics are unstable in the spatiotemporal domain.

For the proof, see Brock and Xepapadeas (2008, Theorem 1).

The eigenvalues of the Jacobian matrix in (70) are given by

$$\lambda_{1,2}\left(k^2\right) = \frac{1}{2}\left(\rho \pm \sqrt{\rho^2 - 4h\left(k^2\right)}\right), \quad k = \frac{2n\pi}{L} \tag{71}$$

$$h\left(k^2\right) = -D^2k^4 + D\left(2H^0_{yp} - \rho\right)k^2 + \det J^0. \tag{72}$$

The conditions of the theorem state that in the parameter space – the Turing space – in which these conditions are satisfied, there exists a diffusivity $D > 0$ and a node n such that both $\lambda_{1,2}\left(k^2\right)$ are positive, while for $D = 0$, the eigenvalues have opposite signs, since $\det J^0 < 0$. The emergence of optimal Turing instability requires that $h\left(k^2\right) > 0$ for some k.

From (71)–(72), diffusion will act as a stabilizer if $\det J^0 = \alpha\left(\rho - \alpha\right) - \beta > 0$ and

$$h\left(z^2\right) = -z^2 + (2\alpha - \rho)z + \det J^0 < 0.$$

 Subscripts associated with functions denote partial derivatives.

D is chosen such that $z = D(2\pi/L)$. This choice will stabilize all nodes $n \geq 1$.

Appendix E

Consider a LQP like (52)–(55) with the following structure:

$$\max_{u(t,x)} \int_0^L \int_0^\infty e^{-\rho t} \left[-\frac{A}{2} y(t,x)^2 - \frac{B}{2} u(t,x)^2 + N y(t,x) u(t,x) \right.$$

$$\left. + \gamma \mathbf{K} y(t,x) \right] dt dx \tag{73}$$

$$A, B, \rho > 0, \ AB - N^2 > 0, \ \mathbf{K}y(t,x) := \int_{\mathcal{O}} w(x - x') y(t, x') dx'$$

$$\text{s.t.} \ \frac{\partial y(t,x)}{\partial t} = Fy(t,x) - Gu(t,x), \ \ F, G > 0 \tag{74}$$

$$y(0,x) = y_0(x) \ \text{given}, \ x \in [0, L] \tag{75}$$

$$y \text{ in a circle } x \in [0, L], y(t,0) = y(x, L) \ \text{for all } t. \tag{76}$$

When $\gamma = 0$, the problem is spatially homogeneous and admits a FOSS. Assume that, as in (52)–(55), the FOSS has the saddle point property. When the spatial effect is introduced by allowing for $\gamma \neq 0$, the Jacobian matrix for the linearization of the Hamiltonian system becomes

$$J^0(y^*, p^*) = \begin{bmatrix} F - \frac{GN}{B} & \frac{G^2}{B} \\ A - \frac{N^2}{B} & \rho - F + \frac{GN}{B} - \gamma \mathbf{K} \end{bmatrix}, \mathbf{K} = \int_{\mathcal{O}} w(x - x') dx'. \tag{77}$$

The saddle point property for the FOSS implies that $\det J^0(y^*, p^* | \gamma = 0) < 0$. If, for $\mathbf{K} > 0, \gamma \neq 0$, trace $J^0(y^*, p^* | \gamma \neq 0) > 0$ and $\det J^0(y^*, p^* | \gamma \neq 0) > 0$, then this spatial effect – realized though the kernel – will destabilize the stable manifold of the flat earth and patterns will emerge.

Appendix F

Given problem (32), the maximum principle under the symmetry assumptions implies the following first-order necessary conditions for $i = 1, 2$:

$$E_i = \frac{-\alpha w_i}{\mu_i}, i = 1, 2 \tag{78}$$

$$\dot{P}_1 = -BP_1 - DP_1 - \frac{\alpha w_1}{\mu_1} \tag{79}$$

$$\dot{P}_2 = -BP_2 + DP_1 - \frac{\alpha w_2}{\mu_2} \tag{80}$$

$$\dot{\mu}_1 = (\rho + B + D)\mu_1 + c_1 + c_2 P_1 - D\mu_2 \tag{81}$$

$$\dot{\mu}_2 = (\rho + B)\mu_2 + c_1 + c_2 P_2. \tag{82}$$

Proof of Proposition 1

A steady state $(P_1^*, P_2^*, \mu_1^*, \mu_2^*)$, if it exists, will satisfy the nonlinear system (79)–(82) for $\dot{P}_1 = \dot{P}_2 = \dot{\mu}_1 = \dot{\mu}_2 = 0$. Solving at a steady state for μ_1^*, μ_2^* from (81), (82), replacing P_1, P_2 from (79),(80), and subtracting, we obtain

$$(\mu_1^* - \mu_2^*) = \frac{\alpha c_2}{(\rho + B + D)\,\mu_1 B} \left[-\frac{w_2}{\mu_2} - \frac{w_1\,(D - B)}{\mu_1\,(D + B)} \right]. \tag{83}$$

If $c_2 = 0$, then $\mu_1^* = \mu_2^*$ and $\tau_1 = \tau_2$ for $w_1 = w_2$. If $D \geq B$, $c_2 > 0$ and $w_1 = w_2$, then, $|\mu_1| > |\mu_2|$ which implies $0 < \tau_1 < \tau_2$. $\blacksquare$

Proof of Saddle Point Stability

The Jacobian matrix of the linearization of the Hamiltonian system (79)–(82) for constant marginal damages is given by

$$J = \begin{pmatrix} -B - D & 0 & \frac{\alpha w}{\mu_1^2} & 0 \\ D & -B & 0 & \frac{\alpha w}{\mu_2^2} \\ 0 & 0 & B + D + \rho & -D \\ 0 & 0 & 0 & B + \rho \end{pmatrix}.$$

The trace is $\mathrm{tr} J = 2\rho$. Following Dockner (1985), the quantity K is defined as

$$K = \begin{vmatrix} \frac{\partial \dot{P}_1}{\partial P_1} & \frac{\partial \dot{P}_1}{\partial \mu_1} \\ \frac{\partial \dot{\mu}_1}{\partial P_1} & \frac{\partial \dot{\mu}_1}{\partial \mu_1} \end{vmatrix} + \begin{vmatrix} \frac{\partial \dot{P}_2}{\partial P_2} & \frac{\partial \dot{P}_2}{\partial \mu_2} \\ \frac{\partial \dot{\mu}_2}{\partial P_2} & \frac{\partial \dot{\mu}_2}{\partial \mu_2} \end{vmatrix} + 2 \begin{vmatrix} \frac{\partial \dot{P}_1}{\partial P_2} & \frac{\partial \dot{P}_1}{\partial \mu_2} \\ \frac{\partial \dot{\mu}_1}{\partial P_2} & \frac{\partial \dot{\mu}_1}{\partial \mu_2} \end{vmatrix}$$

$$= \begin{vmatrix} -(B + D) & \frac{\alpha w}{\mu_1^2} \\ 0 & B + D + \rho \end{vmatrix} + \begin{vmatrix} -B & \frac{\alpha w}{\mu_2^2} \\ 0 & (\rho + B) \end{vmatrix} + 2 \begin{vmatrix} 0 & 0 \\ 0 & -D \end{vmatrix}$$

$$= -(B + D))(\rho + B + D) - B\,(\rho + B) < 0. \tag{84}$$

From Dockner's Theorem 3, under the assumption $\rho \geq 0$, the conditions (i) $K < 0$ and (ii) $0 < \det J \leq \left(\frac{K}{2}\right)^2$ are necessary and sufficient for the eigenvalues of the Hamiltonian (79)–(82) system to be real, with two being positive and two being negative. Since

$$\left(\frac{K}{2}\right)^2 - \det J = \frac{1}{4}\,[(B + D))(\rho + B + D) - B\,(\rho + B)]^2 > 0,$$

both conditions are satisfied and the steady state is a saddle point. The result can be extended to increasing marginal damages. $\blacksquare$

The Hamiltonian System for Problem (42)

Consider a quadratic damage function for each region with spillover temperature effects

$$v_1(T_1, T_2) = c_1^1 T_1 + \frac{1}{2} c_2^1 T_1^2 + \zeta_1^1 T_2 + \frac{1}{2} \zeta_2^1 T_2^2,$$

$$v_2(T_1, T_2) = c_1^2 T_2 + \frac{1}{2} c_2^2 T_2^2 + \zeta_1^2 T_1 + \frac{1}{2} \zeta_2^2 T_1^2.$$

Then

$$E_i = \frac{-\alpha w_i}{\mu_1 \Lambda_1 + \mu_2 \Lambda_2} \,, i = 1, 2, \tag{85}$$

and

$$\dot{\mu}_1 = (\rho + B + \gamma_1 + \gamma_2)\,\mu_1 - (\gamma_1 + \gamma_2)\,\mu_2 + c_1^1 + c_2^1 T_1 + \zeta_1^2 + \zeta_2^2 T_1$$

$$\dot{\mu}_2 = (\rho + B + \gamma_1)\,\mu_2 - \gamma_1 \mu_1 + c_1^2 + c_2^2 T_2 + \zeta_1^1 + \zeta_2^1 T_2.$$

The temperature dynamics of the Hamiltonian system are obtained by replacing E_i in (39)–(41) with (85). This is a dynamical system which can be analyzed using standard methods.

Appendix G

An Approximate Two-Mode Solution of Problem (45)

Following North (1975a), we consider the two-mode approximation of the temperature function in terms of even-numbered Legendre polynomials

$$\hat{T}(x, t) = T_0(t) + T_2(t) P_2(x) \,, \; P_0(x) = 1, P_2(x) = \frac{(3x^2 - 1)}{2}.$$

Note that

$$\int_{-1}^{1} P_n(x) P_m(x)\, dx = \langle P_n(x), P_m(x) \rangle = \frac{\delta_{nm}}{2n + 1},$$

$$\delta_{nm} = \begin{cases} 0 \text{ for } n \neq m \\ 1 \text{ for } n = m \end{cases}$$

$$\langle P_0(x), P_0(x) \rangle = 2, \langle P_0(x), P_2(x) \rangle = 0,$$

$$\int_{-1}^{1} P_2(x)\, dx = 0, \langle P_2(x), P_2(x) \rangle = \frac{2}{5}.$$

In the temperature dynamics (46), make the substitutions

$$\partial_t \hat{T}(x, t) = \dot{T}_0(t) + \dot{T}_2(t) P_2(x)$$

$$\partial_x \hat{T}(x, t) = T_2(t) \frac{dP_2(x)}{dt} = T_2(t)\, 3x,$$

then set $C = 1$ to simplify notation and multiply first by $P_0(x)$ and then by $P_2(x)$ and integrate both sides from -1 to 1 to obtain the two-mode temperature dynamics

$$\dot{T}_0 = Z_0 - (A + BT_0) + \frac{1}{2} \Lambda \int_{-1}^{1} E(x)\, dx \,, \; Z_0 = \int_{-1}^{1} \frac{1}{2} QS(x)\, a(x)\, dx$$

$$\dot{T}_2 = \frac{5}{2}Z_2 - (B + 6D)T_2 \, , \quad Z_2 = \int_{-1}^{1} \frac{1}{2}QS(x)a(x)P_2(x)\,dx.$$

The current value Hamiltonian for the transformed problem will be

$$\int_{x=-1}^{x=1} \left\{ w(x)\left[\ln y(x) + \alpha\ln E(x) - \upsilon\left[T_0 + T_2P_2(x)\right]^2\right] \right.$$

$$\left. + \mu_0\left[Z_0 - (A + BT_0) + \frac{1}{2}\Lambda\int_{-1}^{1}E(x)\,dx\right] + \mu_2\left[\frac{5}{2}Z_2 - (B + 6D)T_2\right] \right\}dx.$$

From the optimality conditions, we obtain

$$E(x) = \frac{-2w(x)\alpha}{\mu_0\Lambda}$$

$$\dot{\mu}_0 = (\rho + B)\mu_0 + \upsilon T_0$$

$$\dot{\mu}_2 = (\rho + B + 6D)\mu_2 + \frac{2}{5}\upsilon T_2$$

$$\dot{T}_0 = Z_0 - (A + BT_0) + \Lambda\frac{\alpha}{\mu_0}$$

$$\dot{T}_2 = \frac{5}{2}Z_2 - (B + 6D)T_2.$$

Solution of this system will provide the temperature and its shadow cost function across locations as

$$\hat{T}(x,t) = T_0(t) + T_2(t)P_2(x) \, , \quad \hat{\mu}(x,t) = \mu_0(t) + \mu_2(t)P_2(x).$$

References

Acemoglu, D., Akcigit, U., Hanley, D. & Kerr, W. (2016). Transition to clean technology. *Journal of Political Economy*, 124(1), 52–104.

Adda, J., Boucekkine, R. & Thuilliez, J. (2024). Epidemics, mental health and public trust. Working paper. www.researchgate.net/publication/377355964_Epidemics_Mental_Health_and_Public_Trust.

Albers, H. J., Fischer, C. & Sanchirico, J. N. (2010). Invasive species management in a spatially heterogeneous world: Effects of uniform policies. *Resource and Energy Economics*, 32(4), 483–99.

Alexeev, V. A. & Jackson, C. H. (2013). Polar amplification: Is atmospheric heat transport important? *Climate Dynamics*, 41(2), 533–47.

Alexeev, V. A., Langen, P. L. & Bates, J. R. (2005). Polar amplification of surface warming on an aquaplanet in "ghost forcing": Experiments without sea ice feedbacks. *Climate Dynamics*, 24(7), 655–66.

Anderson, E. W., Brock, W. A., Hansen, L. P. & Sanstad, A. (2014). Robust analytical and computational explorations of coupled economic-climate models with carbon-climate response. RDCEP Working Paper no. 13-05.

Anderson, E. W., Hansen, L. P. & Sargent, T. J. (2012). Small noise methods for risk-sensitive/robust economies. *Journal of Economic Dynamics and Control*, 36(4), 468–500.

Anthoff, D. & Tol, R. S. J. (2013). The uncertainty about the social cost of carbon: A composition analysis using FUND. *Climatic Change*, 117, 515–30.

Arino, J. (2020). Mathematical epidemiology in a data-rich world. *Infectious Disease Modelling*, 5, 161–88.

Arnott, R., Hochman, O. & Rausser, G. C. (2008). Pollution and land use: Optimum and decentralization. *Journal of Urban Economics*, 64(2), 390–407.

Augeraud-Véron, E., Boucekkine, R., Gozzi, F., Venditti, A. & Zou, B. (2024). Fifty years of mathematical growth theory: Classical topics and new trends. *Journal of Mathematical Economics*, 111(13), 102966.

Baldwin, R., Forslid, R., Martin, P., Ottaviano G. & Robert-Nicoud, F. (2003). *Economic Geography and Public Policy*, Princeton, NJ: Princeton University Press.

Baldwin, R. E. & Martin, P. (2004). Agglomeration and regional growth. In V. Henderson and J.-F. Thisse, eds., *Handbook of Regional and Urban Economics*, vol. 4, Amsterdam: Elsevier, pp. 2671–711.

Barnett, M., Brock, W. A. & Hansen, L. P. (2020). Pricing uncertainty induced by climate change. *Review of Financial Studies* 33(3), 1024–66.

Barnett, M., Brock, W. A. & Hansen, L. P. (2022). Climate change uncertainty spillover in the macroeconomy. *NBER Macroeconomics Annual* 36(1), 253–320.

Başar, T. & Olsder, G. J. (1995). *Dynamic Noncooperative Game Theory*, 2nd ed., London: Academic Press.

Behringer, S. & Upmann, T. (2014). Optimal harvesting of a spatial renewable resource. *Journal of Economic Dynamics and Control*, 42(C), 105–20.

Bekryaev, R. V., Polyakov I. V. & Alexeev, V. A. (2010). Role of polar amplification in long-term surface air temperature variations and modern Arctic warming. *Journal of Climate*, 23(14), 3888–906.

Belik, V., Geisel, T. & Brockmann, D. (2011). Natural human mobility patterns and spatial spread of infectious diseases. *Physical Review X*, 1(1), 011001.

Bewley, T. (1982). An integration of equilibrium theory and turnpike theory. *Journal of Mathematical Economics*, 10(2–3), 233–67.

Bosetti, V., Carraro, C., Galeotti, M., Massetti, E. & Tavoni, M. (2006). WITCH: A World Induced Technical Change Hybrid model. *Energy Journal*, 27(SI2), 13–37.

Boucekkine, R., Camacho, C. & Fabbri, G. (2013). Spatial dynamics and convergence: The spatial AK model. *Journal of Economic Theory*, 148(6), 2719–36.

Boucekkine, R., Camacho, C. & Zou, B. (2009). Bridging the gap between growth theory and the new economic geography: The spatial Ramsey model. *Macroeconomic Dynamics*, 13(1), 20–45.

Boucekkine, R., Fabbri, G., Federico, S. & Gozzi, F. (2019a). Geographical environmental Kuznets curves: The optimal growth linear-quadratic case. *Mathematical Modelling of Natural Phenomena*, 14(1): article 105.

Boucekkine, R., Fabbri, G., Federico, S. & Gozzi, F. (2019b). Growth and agglomeration in the heterogeneous space: A generalized AK approach. *Journal of Economic Geography*, 19(6), 1287–318.

Boucekkine, R., Fabbri, G., Federico, S. & Gozzi, F. (2022a). Managing spatial linkages and geographic heterogeneity in dynamic models with transboundary pollution. *Journal of Mathematical Economics*, 98, 102577.

Boucekkine, R., Fabbri, G., Federico, S. & Gozzi, F. (2022b). A dynamic theory of spatial externalities. *Games and Economic Behavior,* 132, 133–65.

Broadbridge, P. & Hutchinson, A. J. (2022). Integrable nonlinear reaction-diffusion population models for fisheries. *Applied Mathematical Modelling*, 102, 748–67.

Brock, W. A., Engström, G., Grass, D. & Xepapadeas, A. (2013). Energy balance climate models and general equilibrium optimal mitigation policies. *Journal of Economic Dynamics and Control*, 37(12), 2371–96.

Brock, W. A., Engström, G. & Xepapadeas, A. (2014). Spatial climate–economic models in the design of optimal climate policies across locations. *European Economic Review*, 69(C), 78–103.

Brock, W. A., Engström, G. & Xepapadeas, A. (2015). Energy balance climate models, damage reservoirs, and the time profile of climate change policy. In L. Bernard and W. Semmler, eds., *The Oxford Handbook of the Macroeconomics of Global Warming*, Oxford: Oxford University Press, pp. 19–52.

Brock, W. A. & Hansen, L. P. (2019). Wrestling with uncertainty in climate economic models. Working Paper, https://papers.ssrn.com/sol3/papers.cfm?abstract_id=3008833.

Brock, W. A. & Starrett, D. (2003). Managing systems with non-convex positive feedback. *Environmental and Resource Economics*, 26(4), 575–602.

Brock, W. A. & Xepapadeas, A. (2002). Optimal ecosystem management when species compete for limiting resources. *Journal of Environmental Economics and Management*, 44(2), 189–230.

Brock, W. A. & Xepapadeas, A. (2005). Spatial analysis in descriptive models of renewable resource management. *Swiss Journal of Economics and Statistics*, 141(III), 331–54.

Brock, W. A. & Xepapadeas, A. (2008). Diffusion-induced instability and pattern formation in infinite horizon recursive optimal control. *Journal of Economic Dynamics and Control*, 32(9), 2745–87.

Brock, W. A. & Xepapadeas, A. (2010). Pattern formation, spatial externalities and regulation in coupled economic–ecological systems. *Journal of Environmental Economics and Management*, 59(2), 149–64.

Brock, W. A. & Xepapadeas, A. (2017). Climate change policy under polar amplification. *European Economic Review*, 94(C), 263–82.

Brock, W. A. & Xepapadeas, A. (2018). Modeling coupled climate, ecosystems, and economic systems. In P. Dasgupta, S. K. Pattanayak and V. K. Smith, eds., *Handbook of Environmental Economics*, vol. 4, Amsterdam: North-Holland, pp. 1–45.

Brock, W. A. & Xepapadeas, A. (2019). Regional climate change policy under positive feedbacks and strategic interactions. *Environmental and Resource Economics*, 72(1), 51–75.

Brock, W. A. & Xepapadeas, A. (2020). Spatial heat transport, polar amplification and climate change policy. In G. Chichilnisky and A. Rezai, eds., *Handbook of Climate Change*, Cheltenham: Edward Elgar Publishing, pp. 127–66.

Brock, W. & Xepapadeas, A. (2025). Land-use, climate change and the emergence of infectious diseases: A synthesis. *Environmental and Resource Economics*. doi.org/10.1007/s10640-024-00949-9.

Brock, W. A., Xepapadeas, A. & Yannacopoulos, A. N. (2013). Robust control of a spatially distributed commercial fishery. In E. Moser, W. Semmler, G. Tragler and V. M. Veliov, eds., *Dynamic Optimization in Environmental Economics*, Berlin: Springer-Verlag, pp. 215–41.

Brock, W. A., Xepapadeas, A. & Yannacopoulos, A. N. (2014a). Optimal agglomerations in dynamic economics. *Journal of Mathematical Economics*, 53(C), 1–15.

Brock, W. A., Xepapadeas, A. & Yannacopoulos, A. N. (2014b). Optimal control in space and time and the management of environmental resources. *Annual Reviews in Resource Economics*, 6(1), 33–68.

Brock, W. A., Xepapadeas, A. & Yannacopoulos, A. N. (2014c). Robust control and hot spots in spatiotemporal economic systems. *Dynamic Games and Applications*, 4(3), 257–89.

Brock, W. A., Xepapadeas, A. & Yannacopoulos, A. N. (2014d). Spatial externalities and agglomeration in a competitive industry. *Journal of Economic Dynamics and Control*, 42(C), 143–74.

Brozović, N., Sunding, D. & Zilberman, D. (2010). On the spatial nature of the groundwater pumping externality. *Resource and Energy Economics*, 32(2), 154–64.

Cai, Y., Brock, W., Xepapadeas, A. & Judd, K. (2019). Climate policy under spatial heat transport: Cooperative and noncooperative regional outcomes. https://arxiv.org/pdf/1909.04009.pdf.

Cai, Y., Brock, W. & Xepapadeas, A. (2023). Climate change impact on economic growth: Regional climate policy under cooperation and non-cooperation. *Journal of the Association of Environmental and Resource Economists*, 10(3), 569–605.

Calvo, E. & Rubio, S. J. (2012). Dynamic models of international environmental agreements: A differential game approach. *International Review of Environmental and Resource Economics*, 6(4), 289–339.

Camacho, C. & Pérez-Barahona, A. (2015). Land use dynamics and the environment. *Journal of Economic Dynamics and Control*, 52(C), 96–118.

Cantrell, R. S. & Cosner, C. (2003). *Spatial Ecology via Reaction-Diffusion Equations*. Chichester: John Wiley and Sons.

Cass, D. & Shell, K. eds. (1976). *The Hamiltonian Approach to Dynamic Economics*. New York: Academic Press.

Castruccio, S., McInerney, D. J., Stein, M. L., Crouch, F. L., Jacob, R. I. & Moyer, E. J. (2014). Statistical emulation of climate model projections based on precomputed GCM runs. *Journal of Climate*, 27(5), 1829–44.

Chincarini, L. & Asherie, N. (2008). An analytical model for the formation of economic clusters. *Regional Science and Urban Economics*, 38(3), 252–70.

Copeland, B. R. (1996). Pollution content tariffs, environmental rent shifting, and the control of cross-border pollution. *Journal of International Economics*, 40(3–4), 459–76.

Copeland, B. R. & Taylor, M. S. (1994). North–South trade and the environment. *Quarterly Journal of Economics*, 109(3), 755–87.

Copeland, B. R. & Taylor, M. S. (1995). Trade and transboundary pollution. *American Economic Review*, 85(4), 716–37.

Cornet, A. & Camacho, C. (2021). Diffusion of soil pollution in an agricultural economy: The emergence of regions, frontiers and spatial patterns. https://ssrn.com/abstract=3977551.

Costello, C. & Polasky, S. (2004). Dynamic reserve site selection. *Resource and Energy Economics*, 26(2), 157–74.

Costello, C. & Polasky, S. (2008). Optimal harvesting of stochastic spatial resources. *Journal of Environmental Economics and Management*, 56(1), 1–18.

Cruz, J. L. and Rossi-Hansberg, E. (2024). The economic geography of global warming. *Review of Economic Studies*, 91(2), 899–939.

Cui, R., Li, H., Mei, L. & Shi, J. (2017). Effect of harvesting quota and protection zone in a reaction-diffusion model arising from fishery management. *Discrete and Continuous Dynamical Systems - Series B*, 22(3), 791–807.

Deacon, R. T., Kolstad, C. D., Kneese, A. V., Brookshire, D. S., Scrogin, D., Fisher, A. C., Ward, M., Smith, K. & Wilen, J. (1998). Research trends and opportunities in environmental and natural resource economics. *Environmental and Resource Economics*, 11, 383–97.

de Frutos, J. & Martín-Herrán, G. (2019). Spatial effects and strategic behavior in a multiregional transboundary pollution dynamic game. *Journal of Environmental Economics and Management*, 97(C), 182–207.

de Frutos, J., López-Perez, P. M. & Martín-Herrán, G. (2021). Equilibrium strategies in a multiregional transboundary pollution differential game with spatially distributed controls. *Automatica*, 125, 109411.

Denant-Boemont, L., Gaigné, C. & Gaté, R. (2018). Urban spatial structure, transport-related emissions and welfare. *Journal of Environmental Economics and Management*, 89(C), 29–45.

Derzko, N. A., Sethi, S. P. & Thompson, G. L. (1984). Necessary and sufficient conditions for optimal control of quasilinear partial differential systems. *Journal of Optimization Theory and Applications*, 43(1), 89–101.

Desmet, K. & Rossi-Hansberg, E. (2009). Spatial growth and industry age. *Journal of Economic Theory*, 144(6), 2477–502.

Desmet, K. & Rossi-Hansberg, E. (2010). On spatial dynamics. *Journal of Regional Science*, 50(1), 43–63.

Desmet, K. & Rossi-Hansberg, E. (2015). On the spatial economic impact of global warming. *Journal of Urban Economics*, 88(C), 16–27.

Dockner, E. (1985). Local stability analysis in optimal control problems with two variables. In G. Feichtinger, ed., *Optimal Control Theory and Economic Analysis 2*, Amsterdam: North-Holland, pp. 89–113.

Dockner, E. J. & Long, N. V. (1993). International pollution control: Cooperative versus noncooperative strategies. *Journal of Environmental Economics and Management*, 25(1), 13–29.

Dutta, P. & Radner, R. (2006). A game-theoretic approach to global warming. *Advances in Mathematical Economics*, 8, 135–53.

Easterling, W. E. (1997). Why regional studies are needed in the development of full-scale integrated assessment modelling of global change processes. *Global Environmental Change*, 1(4), 337–56.

Epanchin-Nieli, R. S. & Wilen, J. E. (2012). Optimal spatial control of biological invasions. *Journal of Environmental Economics and Management*, 63(2), 260–70.

Ferraccioli, F., Stilianakis, N. I. & Veliov, V. M. (2024). A spatial epidemic model with contact and mobility restrictions. *Mathematical and Computer Modelling of Dynamical Systems*, 30(1), 284-302.

Flannery, B. P. (1984). Energy balance models incorporating transport of thermal and latent energy. *Journal of the Atmospheric Sciences*, 41(3), 414–21.

Francis, J. A. (2017). Why are Arctic linkages to extreme weather still up in the air? *Bulletin of the American Meteorological Society*, 98(12), 2551–57.

Francis, J. A. & Skific, N. (2015). Evidence linking rapid Arctic warming to mid-latitude weather patterns. *Philosophical Transactions of the Royal Society A*, 373(2045), 20140170.

Francis, J. A., Skific, N. & Vavrus, S. J. (2018). North American weather regimes are becoming more persistent: Is Arctic amplification a factor? *Geophysical Research Letters*, 45(20), 11414–22.

Francis, J. A. & Vavrus, S. J. (2014). Evidence for a wavier jet stream in response to rapid Arctic warming. *Environmental Research Letters*, 10(1), 014005.

Fujita, M., Krugman, P. & Venables, A. J. (1999). *The Spatial Economy*, Cambridge, MA: MIT Press.

Fujita, M. & Mori, T. (2005). Frontiers of the new economic geography. *Papers in Regional Science*, 84(3), 377–405.

Fujita, M. & Ogawa, H. (1982). Multiple equilibria and structural transition of non-monocentric urban configurations. *Regional Science and Urban Economics*, 12(2), 161–96.

Fujita, M. & Thisse, J.-F. (2013). *The Economics of Agglomeration: Cities, Industrial Location and Globalization*, 2nd ed., Cambridge: Cambridge University Press.

Gasparrini, A., Guo, Y., Hashizume, M. et al. (2015). Mortality risk attributable to high and low ambient temperature: A multicountry observational study. *The Lancet*, 386(9991), 369–75.

Ghil, M. (1976). Climate stability for a sellers-type model. *Journal of the Atmospheric Sciences*, 33(1), 3–20.

Ghil, M. & Lucarini, V. (2020). The physics of climate variability and climate change. *Reviews of Modern Physics*, 92, 1–77.

Gisser, M. & Sanchez, D. A. (1980). Competition versus optimal control in groundwater pumping. *Water Resources Research*, 16(4), 638–42.

Goetz, R. U. & Zilberman, D. (2000). The dynamics of spatial pollution: The case of phosphorus runoff from agricultural land. *Journal of Economic Dynamics and Control*, 24(1), 143–63.

Goetz, R. U. & Zilberman, D. (2007). The economics of land-use regulation in the presence of an externality: A dynamic approach. *Optimal Control Applications and Methods*, 28(1), 21–43.

Gozzi, F. & Leocata, M. (2022). A stochastic model of economic growth in time-space. *SIAM Journal on Control and Optimization*, 60(2), 620-51.

Grass, D. & Uecker, H. (2017). Optimal management and spatial patterns in a distributed shallow lake model. *Electronic Journal of Differential Equations*, 2017(1), 1–21.

Hansen, L. P. & Sargent, T. J. (2001). Robust control and model uncertainty. *American Economic Review*, 91(2), 60–6.

Hansen, L. P. & Sargent, T. J. (2008). *Robustness in Economic Dynamics*. Princeton, NJ: Princeton University Press.

Hansen, L. P. & Sargent, T. J. (2019). Macroeconomic uncertainty prices when beliefs are tenuous. NBER Working Paper no. 25781. National Bureau of Economic Research, Cambridge, MA.

Hansen, L. P., Sargent, T. J., Turmuhambetova, G. & Williams, N. (2006). Robust control and model misspecification. *Journal of Economic Theory*, 128(1), 45–90.

Hassler, J. & Krusell, P. (2018). Environmental macroeconomics: The case of climate change. In P. Dasgupta, S. K. Pattanayak and V. K. Smith, eds., *Handbook of Environmental Economics*, vol. 4, Amsterdam: North-Holland., pp. 333–94.

Hassler, J., Krusell, P. & Smith, A. A. (2016). Environmental macroeconomics. In J. B. Taylor and H. Uhlig, eds., *Handbook of Macroeconomics*, vol. 2b, Amsterdam: North-Holland, pp. 1893–2008.

Hastings, A. (1982). Dynamics of a single species in a spatially varying environment: The stabilizing role of high dispersal rates. *Journal of Mathematical Biology*, 16(1), 49–55.

Hastings, A. & Harrison, S. (1994). Metapopulation dynamics and genetics. *Annual Review of Ecology and Statistics*, 25, 167–88.

Hatzipanayotou, P., Lahiri, S. & Michael, M. S. (2002). Can cross-border pollution reduce pollution? *Canadian Journal of Economics*, 35(4), 805–18.

Hatzipanayotou, P., Lahiri, S. & Michael, M. S. (2005). Reforms of environmental policies in the presence of cross-border pollution and public–private clean-up. *Scandinavian Journal of Economics*, 107(2), 315–33.

Henderson, J. V. (1977). Externalities in a spatial context: The case of air pollution. *Journal of Public Economics*, 7(1), 89–110.

Hethcote, H. W. (1989). Three basic epidemiological models. In S. A. Levin, T. G. Hallam and L. J. Gross, eds., *Applied Mathematical Ecology*, Berlin: Springer, pp. 119–44.

Hethcote, H. W. (2000). The mathematics of infectious diseases. *SIAM Review*, 42(4), 599–653.

High-Level Commission on Carbon Prices (2017). *Report of the High-Level Commission on Carbon Prices*, Washington, DC: World Bank.

Hope, C. (2006). The marginal impact of CO2 from PAGE2002: An integrated assessment model incorporating the IPCC's five reasons for concern. *Integrated Assessment Journal*, 6(1), 566–77.

Hoyle, R. (2006). *Pattern Formation. An Introduction to Methods*. Cambridge: Cambridge University Press.

Hsiang, S., Kopp, R., Jina, A. et al. (2017). Estimating economic damage from climate change in the United States. *Science*, 356(6345), 1362–69.

Ioannides, Y. M. & Overman, H. G. (2007). Spatial evolution and the U.S. urban system. *Journal of Economic Geography*, 4(2), 131–56.

IPCC (2013). *Climate Change 2013: The Physical Science Basis. Contribution of Working Group I to the Fifth Assessment Report of the Intergovernmental Panel on Climate Change*, T, F. Stocker, D. Qin, G.-K.r Plattner et al., eds., Cambridge: Cambridge University Press.

IPCC (2021). *Climate Change 2021: The Physical Science Basis. Contribution of Working Group I to the Sixth Assessment Report of the Intergovernmental Panel on Climate Change*, V. Masson-Delmotte, P. Zhai, A. Piraniet et al., eds., Cambridge: Cambridge University Press.

Jorgensen, S., Martín-Herrán, G. & Zaccour, G. (2010). Dynamic games in the economics and management of pollution. *Environmental Modeling and Assessment*, 15(6), 443–67.

Kaitala, V., Pohjola, M. & Tahvonen, O. (1992). Transboundary air pollution and soil acidification: A dynamic analysis of an acid rain game between Finland and the USSR. *Environmental and Resource Economics*, 2(2), 161–81.

Kamien, M. I. & Schwartz, N. L. (1991). *Dynamic Optimization: The Calculus of Variations and Optimal Control in Economics and Management*, 2nd ed., Amsterdam: Elsevier.

Kendall, D. G. (1957). Discussion of 'Measles periodicity and community size' by M. S. Bartlett. *Journal of the Royal Statistical Society,* A120, 64–76.

Kendall, D. G. (1965). Mathematical models of the spread of infection. In: *Mathematics and Computer Science in Biology and Medicine*, London: Medical Research Council, pp. 213–25.

Knutti, R. (2013). Relationship between global emissions and global temperature rise. Working Group I Contribution to the IPCC Fifth Assessment Report. Presentation. https://unfccc.int/sites/default/files/7_knutti.reto .3sed2.pdf.

Knutti, R. & Rogelj, J. (2015). The legacy of our CO_2 emissions: A clash of scientific facts, politics and ethics. *Climatic Change*, 133(3), 361–73.

Kolstad, C. (1987). Uniformity versus differentiation in regulating externalities. *Journal of Environmental Economics and Management*, 14(4), 386–99.

Kossioris, G., Plexousakis, M. A., Xepapadeas, A. & de Zeeuw, A. (2011). On the optimal taxation of common-pool resources. *Journal of Economic Dynamics and Control*, 35(11), 1868–79.

Kossioris, G., Plexousakis, M. A., Xepapadeas, A., de Zeeuw, A. & Mäler, K.-G. (2008). Feedback Nash equilibria for non-linear differential games in pollution control. *Journal of Economic Dynamics and Control*, 32(4), 1312–31.

Krugman, P. R. (1996). *The Self-Organizing Economy*, Cambridge, MA: Blackwell Publishers.

Krugman, P. R. (1998). Space: The final frontier. *Journal of Economic Perspectives*, 12(2), 161–74.

Krusell, P. & Smith, A. A. (2022). Climate change around the world. NBER Working Paper no. 30338 and CEPR Discussion Paper no. 17522.

Kurz, M. (1968). The general instability of a class of competitive growth processes. *Review of Economic Studies*, 35(2), 155–74.

Kuwayama, Y. & Brozović, N. (2013). The regulation of a spatially heterogeneous externality: Tradable groundwater permits to protect streams. *Journal of Environmental Economics and Management*, 66(2), 364–82.

Kyriakopoulou, E. & Xepapadeas, A. (2013). Environmental policy, first nature advantage and the emergence of economic clusters. *Regional Science and Urban Economics*, 43(1), 101–16.

Kyriakopoulou, E. & Xepapadeas, A. (2017). Atmospheric pollution in rapidly growing industrial cities: Spatial policies and land use patterns. *Journal of Economic Geography*, 17(3), 607–34.

Langen, P. L. & Alexeev, V. A. (2007). Polar amplification as a preferred response in an idealized aquaplanet GCM. *Climate Dynamics*, 29(2–3), 305–17.

La Torre, D., Liuzzi, D. & Marsiglio, S. (2015). Pollution diffusion and abatement activities across space and over time. *Mathematical Social Sciences*, 78, 48–63.

La Torre, D., Liuzzi, D. & Marsiglio, S. (2021). Transboundary pollution externalities: Think globally, act locally? *Journal of Mathematical Economics*, 96, 102511.

La Torre, D., Liuzzi, D. & Marsiglio, S. (2022). Geographical heterogeneities and externalities in an epidemiological-macroeconomic framework. *Journal of Public Economic Theory*, 24(5), 1154–81.

La Torre, D., Liuzzi, D. & Marsiglio, S. (2024). Epidemic outbreaks and the optimal lockdown area: A spatial normative approach. *Economic Theory*, 77(1), 349–411.

Leduc, M., Matthews, H. D. & de Elía, R. (2016). Regional estimates of the transient climate response to cumulative CO2 emissions. *Nature Climate Change*, 6(5), 474–78.

Lenton, T. M., Held, H., Kriegler, E. et al. (2008). Tipping elements in the Earth's climate system. *PNAS*, 105(6), 1786–93.

Levin, S. A. (1974). Dispersion and population interactions. *American Naturalist*, 108(960), 207–28.

Levin, S. A. (1976). Population dynamic models in heterogeneous environments. *Annual Review of Ecology and Systematics*, 7(1), 287–310.

Levin, S. A. & Segel, L. A. (1985). Pattern generation in space and aspect. *SIAM Review*, 27(1), 45–67.

Levin, S. A. & Xepapadeas, A. (2017). Transboundary capital and pollution flows and the emergence of regional inequalities. *Discrete and Continuous Dynamical Systems - Series B*, 22(3), 913-22.

Lin, J., Andreasen, V., Casagrandi, R. & Levin, S. A. (2003). Traveling waves in a model of influenza A drift. *Journal of Theoretical Biology*, 222(4), 437–45.

Liu, Y. & Sims, C. (2016). Spatial-dynamic externalities and coordination in invasive species control. *Resource and Energy Economics*, 44, 23–38.

Lucas, R. E., Jr. (2001). Externalities and cities. *Review of Economic Dynamics*, 4(2), 245–74.

Lucas, R. E., Jr. & Rossi-Hansberg, E. (2002). On the internal structure of cities. *Econometrica*, 70(4), 1445–76.

MacDougall, A. H. & Friedlingstein, P. (2015). The origin and limits of the near proportionality between climate warming and cumulative CO2 emissions. *Journal of Climate*, 28(10), 4217–30.

MacDougall, A. H., Swart, N. C. & Knutti, R. (2017). The uncertainty in the transient climate response to cumulative CO2 emissions arising from the uncertainty in physical climate parameters. *Journal of Climate*, 30(2), 813–27.

Mäler, K.-G. (1989). The acid rain game. In H. Folmer and E. van Ierland, eds., *Valuation Methods and Policy Making in Environmental Economics*, vol. 36, Amsterdam: Elsevier, pp. 231–52.

Mäler, K.-G. & de Zeeuw, A. (1998). The acid rain differential game. *Environmental and Resource Economics*, 12(2), 167–84.

Mäler, K.-G., Xepapadeas, A. & de Zeeuw, A. (2003). The economics of shallow lakes. *Environmental and Resource Economics*, 26(4), 603–24.

Matthews, H. D., Gillett, N. P, Stott, P. A. & Zickfield, K. (2009). The proportionality of global warming to cumulative carbon emissions. *Nature*, 459(7248), 829–33.

Matthews, H. D., Solomon, S. & Pierrehumbert, R. (2012). Cumulative carbon as a policy framework for achieving climate stabilization. *Philosophical Transactions of the Royal Society A*, 370, 4365–79.

McKenzie, L. W. (1976). Turnpike theory. *Econometrica*, 44(5), 841–65.

Merlis, T. M. & Henry, M. (2018). Simple estimates of polar amplification in moist diffusive energy balance models. *Journal of Climate*, 31(15), 5811–24.

Milner, F. A. & Zhao, R. (2008). S-I-R model with directed spatial diffusion. *Mathematical Population Studies*, 15(3), 160-81.

Murray, J. D. (2002). *Mathematical Biology, I: An Introduction*, 3rd ed., Berlin: Springer.

Murray, J. D. (2003). *Mathematical Biology, II: Spatial Models and Biomedical Applications*, 3rd ed., Berlin: Springer.

Nagase, Y. & Silva, E. C. D. (2007). Acid rain in China and Japan: A game-theoretic analysis. *Regional Science and Urban Economics*, 37(1), 100–20.

Negri, D. H. (1989). The common property aquifer as a differential game. *Water Resources Research*, 25(1), 9–15.

Nordhaus, W. D. (2011). Estimates of the social cost of carbon: Background and results from the RICE-2011 model. NBER Working Paper no. 17540. National Bureau of Economic Research, Cambridge, MA.

Nordhaus, W. D. (2014). Estimates of the social cost of carbon: Concepts and results from the DICE-2013R model and alternative approaches. *Journal of the Association of Environmental and Resource Economists*, 1(1/2), 273–312.

Nordhaus, W. D. (2017). Revisiting the social cost of carbon. *Proceedings of the National Academy of Sciences*, 114(7), 1518–23.

Nordhaus, W. D. & Sztorc, P. (2013). *DICE 2013-R: Introduction and User's Manual*, Yale University, New Haven, CT.

Nordhaus, W. D. & Yang, Z. (1996). A regional dynamic general-equilibrium model of alternative climate-change strategies. *American Economic Review*, 86(4), 741–65.

North, G. R. (1975a). Analytical solution to a simple climate model with diffusive heat transport. *Journal of the Atmospheric Sciences*, 32(7), 1301–07.

North, G. R. (1975b). Theory of energy-balance climate models. *Journal of the Atmospheric Sciences*, 32(11), 2033–43.

North, G. R., Cahalan, R. F. & Coakley, J. A. Jr. (1981). Energy balance climate models. *Reviews of Geophysics and Space Physics*, 19(1), 91–121.

North, G. R. & Kim, K.-Y. (2017). *Energy Balance Climate Models*. Hoboken, NJ: Wiley.

Pfeiffer, L. & Lin, C. Y. (2012). Groundwater pumping and spatial externalities in agriculture. *Journal of Environmental Economics and Management*, 64(1), 16–30.

Pindyck, R. S. (2007). Uncertainty in environmental economics. *Review of Environmental Economics and Policy*, 1(1), 45–65.

Pindyck, R. S. (2011). Fat tails, thin tails, and climate change policy. *Review of Environmental Economics and Policy*, 5(2), 258–74.

Pindyck, R. S. (2012). Uncertain outcomes and climate change policy. *Journal of Environmental Economics and Management*, 63(3), 289–303.

Pindyck, R. S. (2013). Climate change policy: What do the models tell us? *Journal of Economic Literature*, 51(3), 860–72.

Provencher, B. & Burt, O. (1993). The externalities associated with the common property exploitation of groundwater. *Journal of Environmental Economics and Management*, 24(2), 139–58.

Quah, D. T. (1996). Empirics for economic growth and convergence. *European Economic Review*, 40(6), 1353–75.

Quah, D. T. (1997). Empirics for growth and distribution: Stratification, polarization, and convergence clubs. *Journal of Economic Growth*, 2(1), 27–59.

Quah, D. T. (2002). Spatial agglomeration dynamics. *AEA Papers and Proceedings*, 92(2), 247–52.

Ramanathan, V., Crutzen, P. J., Mitra, A. P. & Sikka, D. (2002). The Indian Ocean experiment and the Asian brown cloud. *Current Science*, 83(8), 947–54.

Rassweiler, A., Costello, C. & Siegel, D. A. (2012). Marine protected areas and the value of spatially optimized fishery management. *Proceedings of the National Academy of Sciences*, 109(29), 11884–9.

Redding, S. J. & Rossi-Hansberg, E. (2017). Quantitative spatial economics. *Annual Review of Economics*, 9(1), 21–58.

Regnier, C. & Legras, S. (2018). Urban structure and environmental externalities. *Environmental and Resource Economics*, 70(1), 31–52.

Rossi-Hansberg, E. & Sarte, P.-D. (2012). Economics of housing externalities. *International Encyclopedia of Housing and Home*, 2, 47–50.

Rossi-Hansberg, E., Sarte, P.-D. & Owens, R. III. (2010). Housing externalities. *Journal of Political Economy*, 118(3), 485–535.

Ruan, S. (2007). Spatial-temporal dynamics in nonlocal epidemiological models. In Y. Takeuchi, Y. Iwasa and K. Sato, eds., *Mathematics for Life Science and Medicine*, Berlin: Springer, pp. 97–122.

Saak, A. E. & Peterson, J. M. (2007). Groundwater use under incomplete information. *Journal of Environmental Economics and Management*, 54(2), 214–28.

Sanchirico, J. N. (2005). Additivity properties of metapopulation models: Implications for the assessment of marine reserves. *Journal of Environmental Economics and Management*, 49(1), 1–25.

Sanchirico, J. N. & Wilen, J. E. (1999). Bioeconomics of spatial exploitation in a patchy environment. *Journal of Environmental Economics and Management*, 37(2), 129–50.

Sanchirico, J. N. & Wilen, J. E. (2001). A bioeconomic model of marine reserve creation. *Journal of Environmental Economics and Management*, 42(3), 257–76.

Sanchirico, J. N. & Wilen, J. E. (2005). Optimal spatial management of renewable resources: Matching policy scope to ecosystem scale. *Journal of Environmental Economics and Management*, 50(1), 23–46.

Schindler, M., Caruso, G. & Picard, P. (2017). Equilibrium and first-best city with endogenous exposure to local air pollution from traffic. *Regional Science and Urban Economics*, 62(C), 12–23.

Sellers, W. D. (1969). A global climatic model based on the energy balance of the Earth-atmosphere system. *Journal of Applied Meteorology*, 8(3), 392–440.

Sigman, H. (2005). Transboundary spillovers and decentralization of environmental policies. *Journal of Environmental Economics and Management*, 50(1), 82–101.

Silva, E. C. D. & Caplan, A. J. (1997). Transboundary pollution control in federal systems. *Journal of Environmental Economics and Management*, 34(2), 173–86.

Smith, M. D., Sanchirico, J. N. & Wilen, J. E. (2009). The economics of spatial-dynamic processes: Applications to renewable resources. *Journal of Environmental Economics and Management*, 57(1), 104–21.

Smith, M. D. & Wilen, J. E. (2003). Economic impacts of marine reserves: The importance of spatial behavior. *Journal of Environmental Economics and Management*, 46(2), 183–206.

Stiglitz, J. E. (2019). Addressing climate change through price and non-price interventions. *European Economic Review*, 119, 594–612.

Tsangaris, S., Xepapadeas, A., Yannacopoulos, A. N. & Salvati, L. (2024). Spatial externalities, R&D spillovers, and endogenous technological change. *Regional Science and Urban Economics*, 109, 104055.

Turing, A. M. (1952). The chemical basis of morphogenesis. *Philosophical Transactions of the Royal Society of London B*, 237(641), 37–72.

Uecker, H. (2016). Optimal harvesting and spatial patterns in a semiarid vegetation system. *Natural Resource Modeling*, 29(2), 229–58.

Ulph, A. (1997). International trade and the environment: A survey of recent economic analysis. In H. Folmer and T. Tietenberg, eds., *The International Yearbook of Environmental and Resource Economics 1997/1998: A Survey of Current Issues*, Cheltenham: Edward Elgar, pp. 205–42.

van der Ploeg, F. & de Zeeuw, A. J. (1992). International aspects of pollution control. *Environmental and Resource Economics*, 2(2), 117–39.

Verhoef, E. T. & Nijkamp, P. (2002). Externalities in urban sustainability: Environmental versus localization-type agglomeration externalities in a general spatial equilibrium model of a single-sector monocentric industrial city. *Ecological Economics*, 40(2), 157–79.

Verhoef, E. T. & Nijkamp, P. (2003). Externalities in the urban economy. Tinbergen Institute Discussion Paper no. 2003-078/3. https://ssrn.com/abstract=457580.

Verhoef, E. T. & Nijkamp, P. (2005). Spatial externalities and the urban economy. In R. Capello and P. Nijkamp, eds., *Urban Dynamics and Growth:*

Advances in Urban Economics, Leeds: Emerald Group Publishing Limited, pp. 88–120.

Voss, R., Quaas, M. F., Schmidt, J. O. et al. (2018). Quantifying the benefits of spatial fisheries management: An ecological-economic optimization approach. *Ecological Modelling*, 385, 165–72.

Wagener, F. O. O. (2003). Skiba points and heteroclinic bifurcations, with applications to the shallow lake system. *Journal of Economic Dynamics and Control*, 27(9), 1533–61.

Wilen, J. E. (2007). Economics of spatial-dynamic processes. *American Journal of Agricultural Economics*, 89(5), 1134–44.

Wu, B. & Francis, J. A. (2019). Summer Arctic cold anomaly dynamically linked to East Asian heat waves. *Journal of Climate*, 30(4), 1137–50.

Xabadia, A., Goetz, R. & Zilberman, D. (2004). Optimal dynamic pricing of water in the presence of waterlogging and spatial heterogeneity of land. *Water Resources Research*, 40(7), W07S02.

Xabadia, A., Goetz, R. & Zilberman, D. (2006). Control of accumulating stock pollution by heterogeneous producers. *Journal of Economic Dynamics and Control*, 30(7), 1105–30.

Xabadia, A., Goetz, R. & Zilberman, D. (2008). The gains from differentiated policies to control stock pollution when producers are heterogeneous. *American Journal of Agricultural Economics*, 90(4), 1059–63.

Xepapadeas, A. (2022). On the optimal management of environmental stock externalities. *Proceedings of the National Academy of Sciences*, 119(24), e2202679119.

Xepapadeas, A. & Yannacopoulos, A. N. (2016). Spatial growth with exogenous saving rates. *Journal of Mathematical Economics*, 67, 125–37.

Xepapadeas, A. & Yannacopoulos, A. N. (2023). Spatial growth theory: Optimality and spatial heterogeneity. *Journal of Economic Dynamics and Control*, 146, 104584.

Yang, Z. (2008). *Strategic Bargaining and Cooperation in Greenhouse Gas Mitigations: An Integrated Assessment Modeling Approach*. Cambridge, MA: MIT Press.

most pressing environmental, natural resource, and sustainability challenges. Bridging economics, ecology, decision theory, and policy, each volume synthesizes cutting-edge research, theoretical and mathematical insights, and practical case studies. Designed for academics, policymakers, and advanced students, the series explores key topics such as climate economics, biodiversity conservation, social cost-benefit analysis, sustainable development, decision theory and policy design for sustainable economic transformations–all presented in a rigorous yet approachable format. With a global perspective and contributions from a diverse community of top scholars, the series equips readers with the knowledge, models, and tools needed to understand and help shape the transition toward a sustainable relationship between nature, the economy, and society–one of the defining challenges of the 21st century.

Theory and Methods for Environmental, Natural Resource and Sustainable Development Economics

- AI, Machine Learning
- Cost Benefit Analysis
- Decision Theory, Uncertainty, Ambiguity
- Discounting
- Economic Instrument and Policy Design
- Experimental and Behavior Approaches
- Financial Economics and Econometrics
- Game Theory and Agent-based modelling
- General Equilibrium Analysis and Impact Assessment Models
- Macroeconomic and Microeconomic Modelling
- Non-Linearities and Tipping Points
- Open Science, Open Data, Digitalization
- Sustainable Business Modelling and ESG Strategies
- Sustainable Development: Modelling, Measurement, Pathways
- Time Series, Spatial, Panel Econometrics
- Valuation Methods

Thematic Areas for Environmental, Natural Resources and Sustainable Development Economics and Econometrics

- Biodiversity
- Circular Economy
- Energy
- Land Use and Land Use Change
- Marine Use
- Natural Resources Management
- Transport
- Water

For EU product safety concerns, contact us at Calle de José Abascal, 56–1°, 28003 Madrid, Spain or eugpsr@cambridge.org.